Ashes in the Mouth

The story of the Bodyline Tour
1932–33

Ronald Mason

THE HAMBLEDON
PRESS

THE HAMBLEDON PRESS
35 GLOUCESTER AVENUE
LONDON NW1 7AX

1982

ISBN 0 907628 31 1

British Library Cataloguing in Publication Data
Mason, Ronald
    Ashes in the mouth: the story of the bodyline tour 1932-3.
    1. Cricket − Australia
    2. Cricket − England
    I. Title
    796. 35' 865   GV928. A8

Printed and bound in Great Britain by
Robert Hartnoll Ltd, Bodmin, Cornwall

CONTENTS

ACKNOWLEDGEMENTS

This book was planned some time ago; the unexpected but unavoidable delays in publication have neatly and happily ensured that its appearance coincides with the jubilee, if that is really the word, of the historic events chronicled. The delay has also meant that I have had more cheerful and friendly encouragement and assistance than I could possibly have had if all had gone smoothly from the start; I wish I could list by name everyone who has helped me with advice and suggestions. This would hardly be practicable; but my thanks must certainly be recorded to Ellen Dudson who typed the entire script, so long ago that it will be a shock to her to see it in print: to Kay Saunders and Peter Hill without whose efforts this book would not have been published: to Colin Johnston, my Australian friend, who carried out certain valuable researches and enquiries for me: to Scyld Berry and Benny Green for making kind and unsolicited recommendations at certain stages: to my son Nick, who as always came both professionally and filially to my aid when approached: and to my wife for being as patient and indulgent as ever for a rather longer time than usual.

There are two others of whom special mention must be made, for they were both prominent members of the illustrious touring team itself: these were Messrs. G.O. Allen and R.E.S. Wyatt. Each of them readily gave up time to read through the text, and in each case made considered and very valuable suggestions as to emendations and additions. They could not have been more helpful and generous — but wait, the last-mentioned could be and was, for he has written the introduction too. I am very grateful to both of them; they have added a *cachet* to the volume that it would otherwise have lacked.

Ronald Mason
Banstead, 1982

LIST OF PLATES
(Between pages 118 and 119)

INTRODUCTION

by R.E.S. WYATT

I first met Ronald Mason nearly 60 years ago in the classroom at my uncle's prep school during my first match at Lord's when I was embarking on a first class cricket career and he was a small boy being taught Latin grammar by my uncle. Nearly 40 years passed before we met again at Lord's during a Test Match by which time he had made his name as an author. I believe in one of his books on cricket he describes how our first meeting helped to instil in him an even greater love for the game. If this is true I might claim a little credit for the enchancement of cricket literature. Mr. Mason has written numerous books, several of which are on cricket. I am always impressed by his command of the English language and his turn of phrase. Not only is he an excellent writer but his knowledge of the game – the tactics and strategy and the methods of attack and defence as applied to both batting and bowling – qualifies him to write intelligently on the subject of the Body-line Tour. In fact I have never met anyone who has not played first class cricket who is more conversant with the finer points of the game. This coupled with his great ability as a writer more than justifies his tackling what I should imagine proved to be a difficult task. He has accomplished this so well that the result is a book of accurate detail and immense interest.

I consider the chapter on Jardine is excellent. The author portrays him so accurately that I almost feel myself to be again in his presence. I am pleased to see tribute paid to his "warmth and charm". Too seldom has he been given credit for these qualities, which he certainly possessed, as he did kindness and generosity.

As vice-captain of the M.C.C. Team I have read the book with a very critical eye. The author's description of how the body-line attack evolved and how it affected the players' attitude and the spirit of the game is perfectly correct. There have been so many misleading stories about various meetings prior to the side leaving England and also on the boat bound for Australia that it is refreshing to read the truth. The account of the Test Matches is vivid and accurate in detail making it enthralling to read. *Ashes in the Mouth* is a cricket story of the most sensational tour of all time by a writer of distinction who writes beautifully with a surprising appreciation of the true facts. This book cannot but help to appeal to cricket lovers who wish to learn more about a very interesting, but what must be admitted to have been an unfortunate tour.

1

PROLOGUE

Everyone remembers how Lillee and Thomson demoralised the English batsmen in the winter of 1974-75 and by so doing inflamed partisan emotions in a manner by no means unprecedented but still traditionally alien to the game. Not only were emotions awakened, but memories were uncomfortably stirred. Over forty years had passed, bowling and fielding techniques had developed, new laws had been introduced and manners and habits altered (not always for the better); but still the strange lurid tour of Australia by the M.C.C. in the winter of 1932-33 lay close indeed to the surface of the memory, however richly the history of subsequent triumphs and tragedies may have seemed to overlay it. Lillee and Thomson were of course by no means the first bowlers in recent history to bring the name of Larwood into comparison, quite often coupled with an opprobrious epithet; a mighty line of fast bowlers from Larwood's day onwards had found the mention of the familiar name an inevitable incident in their public history — Constantine, Martindale, Lindwall, Miller, Tyson, Trueman, Statham, Griffith, Hall come instantly to mind, and now in our own day Roberts, Holding and Garner have intensified the tradition. If any of these bumped the ball at a batsman, and naturally they all did on occasion, some more than others, the ghost of Larwood's body-line tour would rise automatically to be invoked. With Lillee and Thomson in particular it was called back so insistently that the forty-two-year-old memory seemed as powerful an emotive symbol as the contemporary actuality; and those who have carried on this distinctive brand of aggression have kept the image very clearly before us.

It is reasonable to feel that a book of this kind could be projected as a useful topical comparison. I had felt for some time that the years had dimmed the vividness of the original crisis; that assumptions, accurate or otherwise, were hardening into beliefs without adequate reference to the available facts; and that an account, as dispassionate as possible, that reviewed the events as nearly as could be as they occurred might serve to set what I have already described as an emotive symbol into as balanced a perspective as could be achieved. The only fears that I had originated in tentative scruples: would a re-telling serve any positive purpose, have any result other than the unhappy and unnecessary re-awakening of forgotten angers and recriminations? I hesitated for a long time about this, engaged in heart-searching and self-reproach, taking advice from here and there, sheltering from my own uncertainties behind the opinions of others. One illustrious member of Jardine's touring party was, in the friendliest possible way, emphatic in his discouragement. "You've no idea what it was like", he said, "It was diabolical." One of his colleagues, while rejecting that particular word, was inclined to agree with him over inadvisability; but added a significant note that injustice had been done over the years and implied that there was room for something to be put right. In neither of these cases did discouragement imply hostility or non-co-operation. I was grateful for the opinions and took them very much to heart; the fact that I have proceeded with the venture does not mean that I have failed to value the views expressed. I still felt, even in face of these eminent authorities, that an effort could be made to reduce this nebulous and sinister myth to its actual and historical place in the history of the game. With apologies and acknowledgment to all, that is what I have tried to do.

And it must not be forgotten that this tour, elevated (or diminished) in the folk-mind to nothing but a simplified symbol of ruthless conflict between isolated outsize figures of energy, Jardine and Larwood on the one side, Bradman and Woodfull on the other, comprised in fact a far richer variety of character, crisis and achievement than the common memory is encouraged to inherit. If you determine to erase this tour from the consciousness because of the distresses engendered in it, you will erase too certain artistries, heroisms, triumphs that ought not to be forgotten, for their own bright sakes certainly but also for their counterbalancing qualities, their assertion, even in the face of regrettable angers and prejudices and obstinacies, of the saving graces of skill and courage and resource that are implicit in the acknowledged complex greatness of the game itself. High on the list of these I would put Bradman's century in the second innings of the second Test, and not far below it McCabe's superb 187 not out in the first innings of the first; and other names that must not in this context be submerged without honour, for exploits to be recounted in their place, are

Woodfull, Sutcliffe, Hammond, Fingleton, Richardson, O'Reilly and, in his very special niche of fame, Eddie Paynter. The parts played by these, and indeed by many others in less spectacular ways, helped to elevate this series in the eyes of the unbiased observer, if such a phenomenon were possible, into a tough and vital succession of encounters not easily matched in the history of Test cricket and unhappily misrepresented in the common memory because of the eclipsing nature of the central controversy. Statistically, the results show an overwhelming English dominance, varied by one comprehensive defeat, in the second Test at Melbourne; I feel this to be deceptive. None of the matches was run away with: several of the games whose scores speak plainly of England's supremacy contained long periods of combative tension during which nobody would have cared to bet on the outcome; and even Australia's fine win at Melbourne by 111 runs sustained its excited balance until well into its last day. The whole tour has been overshadowed, as is natural, by the fierce outbreaks of publicized rancour that suceeded upon the immediate success of Jardine's tactics. It seems to be worth the attempt to place both those tactics, the occasion for the use of them, and the varied and many-sided characters and skills involved, in their proper relations to their forerunners and to us.

*   *   *

The Body-line tour of 1932-3 was not an isolated incident or an accident of individual temperament. It was in fact a crucially dramatic moment in the development of the history of an important section of the first-class cricket history, namely Anglo-Australian cricket; it later became, and this is a different matter, the root cause of important developments in the techniques and tactics of the game itself, helping to shift the preponderant balance of a style from the off-side to the leg-side, gaining perhaps something in subtlety and resource and losing certainly something in freedom and aesthetic grace. But at present later history can be discounted; it is its origins, obscure and random as they may be, that call for a moment's examination.

They lie, I am persuaded, in the climate of popular response to the progress during the first thirty years of the century of the successive Test series between England and Australia. Test cricket then took up more of the public imagination than can be spared for it today, when football has become an intensive cult, and the age has become less patient and more demanding. In the early 1900s there were only two Test contestants who really mattered, England and Australia; and although by the 1930s South Africa and the West Indies were also established and New Zealand and India had just arrived, none of these "lesser" powers called out the response that was immediately evident when Australia was the opponent. Folk memory and folk emotions die hard; and although the relative strengths of these cricketing nations, to whom Pakistan must now be added as a fiercely competitive rival, bear now very little relation to the length of their respective traditions, it is still true that England and Australia, at least *in* England and Australia, remain the most signal and illustrious rivals, call forth the most intense and universal partisanship, — assisted, in one way and another by the strange, potent and not altogether commendable symbolism of the Ashes. England would rather beat Australia than anybody else; Australia, though in its flat-vowelled accents it may affect to despise the Poms, would I am sure submit gracefully enough to defeat by all or any of the others provided that she could for all that beat England.

In this context, which during the first thirty years of the century was a clean and uncluttered rivalry with nothing comparable to distract it, the triumphs and disasters had fluctuated predictably, but with unremitting tensions involved, up to the outbreak of the First World War; and the accidental fact that the chasm opened while England were in temporary supremacy had a very pronounced effect on their morale when Tests were once again permitted to resume in the 1920s.

The series of 1911-12, followed up by the ambitious but disastrous Triangular Tournament of the next (and wet) summer, had seen a depleted Australia falter before a rampantly aggressive England, endowed for the moment with a small handful of batsmen and bowlers of world class at the top of their form; and this was the invigorating memory from which English cricketers, during the savageries and monotonies of the dreary war years, could draw optimistic sustenance for what they hoped would soon be a peaceful and compensating future. They embarked upon post-war cricket in a mood of relief and confidence, bolstered deceptively by a sunny hard-wicket season in 1920 when runs abounded and the golden age seemed to have returned in all its glory, and set off in high feather for Australia that autumn in the cheerful expectation that the deplorable intermission could now be forgotten, that relations could be resumed immediately on the happy footings of 1912 with England modestly on top, and that God was in his heaven and all was right with the world.

They were there and then, of course, submitted to an unprecedented humiliation, five matches to none. It was by no means a great England side, but it was not a negligible one, and it included at least three of the most resplendent names in the game's whole history, Hobbs, Rhodes and Woolley, and you do not need to stretch very far to squeeze a fourth, Hendren, into their company. Be that as it may, they were crushed, and crushed without mercy, by a compact consortium of youthful vigour and matured experience controlled by a ruthless leader, W.W. Armstrong. The reasons for the discrepancies are many and complex, and extend far wider and deeper than the restricted contexts of the game; interestingly enough, they were predictably duplicated at the end of the Second World War a generation later. This is not the place for a diagnosis, or indeed for more than a self-evident generalisation; but the evidence of each war's aftermath is plain, that English cricket suffered each time far more heavily than Australia's, and that its rebuilding process was each time more prolonged. The great formations that had made historic successes just before the battles could never be reassembled to any comparable effect; whereas the Australians, who had been nearly as far up to the neck in the common dangers as the English, seemed to be able to re-establish their vigour and potentiality overnight. Gregory and McDonald sprang fresh from the first tumult, Lindwall and Miller from the second; England had no comparable immediate discoveries, and it took their younger men several years to find the experience necessary to establish equality

again, let alone ascendancy. By 1946 this was an accepted
pattern; in 1921 it was not, it was a humiliating jolt to the
amour propre of a cricketing nation that had always
instinctively felt itself superior and had now been violently
and rudely assailed with self-doubt. I am not sure how
faithfully the celebrated words of Kipling during the Boer
War applied here — "We have had no end of a lesson: it will do
us no end of good." The first half of the line applied all right,
but the second — ? It is difficult to say. It made those in
control of English cricket tentative, uncertain, scared. In the
next season of 1921 Armstrong's visiting Australians found
England's tottering morale once more unready, dealt it severe
blows, capsized any confidence that the previous winter had
left standing and showed up the selectors as panic- stricken
and directionless, without the courage to back their own
blind guesses. English *cricket* was not destroyed by Armstrong's Australians, far from it; but the serenity and security
of English self-confidence was. Dispassionate observers may
wryly feel that taken for all in all this may ultimately have
been no bad thing; but the doubt persists. We had no end of a
lesson; that was salutary enough. Whether it had done us no
end of good remained, still remains, to be seen.

The strenuous process of rehabilitation continued through
the early 1920s. Some little confidence was restored by
interim victories over South Africa; one world-class batsman
was discovered, Sutcliffe, and one world-class bowler, Tate.
When Gilligan's team went to Australia in the autumn of
1924 the grind was still an uphill one, but the effects of
regrouping and reinforcement were there for encouragement,
and two of the early Tests, though lost, were tough battles

fought to a standstill. The fourth, to everyone's delight, even, I feel, the Australians', signalled England's first Test victory since 1912; ruin and anti-climax, collectively assembled under the name of Grimmett, followed in the fifth, but somehow morale remained at a heightened level; and when Collins brought his team over to England in 1926 and a not very satisfactory rain-bedevilled series was rounded off by a spectacular English victory at the Oval, the accumulated frustrations of more than a dozen years erupted in a nationalistic explosion of wild relief and the unregenerate Anglo-Saxon complacency felt itself once more established in its traditional place of honour

A short period of euphoric content followed this celebrated success; but the less discerning among the enthusiasts were inclined to overlook the fact that what they were watching was not so much the rehabilitation of England as the inevitable disintegration of the great Australian menace of Armstrong's day. McDonald was no longer there; Gregory, Bardsley and Macartney were in the natural order of things less formidable, (though there were classic and prolonged moments when Bardsley and Macartney appeared to contradict this). Certain younger players, Taylor and Andrews in particular, made less progress than they had promised; the whole fearsome combination was reduced to something much more manageable. Sighs of relief were breathed; youth and ebullience, in the engaging person of Percy Chapman, set off cheerfully for Australia in 1928 with a more compact and promising party than Gilligan had been able to command, carrying with him not only the best seam bowler and the best opening batsmen in the world but a newly-fledged all-rounder of immense potentiality and power by the name of Walter Hammond. This time it was the Australians who seemed to be caught on the wrong foot. The first Test at Brisbane capsized them in a disaster matching England's worst post-war predicaments (England won by 675 runs; it is a wry pleasure to record this in the sobering recessions of these latter days) and the second Test at Sydney was almost as decisive a victory. Nevertheless it became plain to the shrewd watcher that wrong foot or not at the beginning, the Australians were perceptibly quicker than the mother country in contriving to get back on to the right one. The next two Tests were classics of their kind, the entrenched and aggressive skills of the English being challenged positively and resourcefully by certain exciting infusions of new blood. Anyone might have won up to the last five minutes of each of these glorious games, Melbourne and Adelaide, January and February 1929, but as it happened England did. They rather deflatingly, not to say ominously, lost the last Test; but arriving home with a four-one victory in the rubber tended not unreasonably to ignore the hard fact that a rapid redressing of balance was taking place before their unseeing eyes, and that a run or two here and a wicket or two there would have clinched the rubber by three to two against them. And there remained after the tumult and the shouting the unavoidable truth that although custom might not have staled the pleasure to the public of the skills of such classic performers as Hobbs, Hendren, White, even Tate, age was nevertheless getting on busily with the process of withering them. True enough, they were not gone yet; and truer and even more to the point, we had found Hammond, whose performances in the Chapman series had firmly stamped him, for the time, as chief candidate for the potential honour of being the world's greatest batsman when Jack Hobbs pleased to step down. For the time, though, for the time; it proved a very short time, for the last few Tests in Australia had revealed the home side as the spirited possessor of surprising powers of re-invigoration. It was still true that they could not yet find destructive spearheads to replace the force that Gregory and McDonald had been in their great years, and their main reliance for the attack was still, as it would be for some time yet, on the ageless genius of Grimmett; but the batting was another matter.

It had been common knowledge before the tour was under way that certain young batsmen of high promise were incubating in the background, and it was not long before their reputations were being reinforced in performance, both in matches against the M.C.C. tourists and in inter-State games. Two in especial had been singled out for notice — foremost of them the graceful and brilliant Archie Jackson, a boy still only nineteen who had secured his place in his State side as many as two seasons earlier and had already established himself not only as a fast and prolific scorer but as a supremely elegant stylist; a modest retiring character who got used very early to seeing his name bracketed in all seriousness with Victor Trumper, a comparison that would in most cases be as frivolous as a comparison in other contexts with Shakespeare or Mozart but which in his case has been honoured rather than scorned by the appraisal of history. The second of the two prominent newcomers, spoken of at the very outset as if he were perhaps the slightly less remarkable talent of the two, did not take very long to display his potentialities either. He was just twenty and his name was Don Bradman, and it is an indication of the frightening potencies of a cricketing community that could produce from its sleeve, when the hour demanded it, two bright stars of which he was considered to be the lesser. Only the sickening misfortune of Jackson's early decline into illness and death has prevented the development of a twin promise without precedent. It is hard to believe that Jackson's future career, had it been allowed to happen, could have matched the world-scale mastery of his fellow's; the imagination, particularly the English imagination, quails before the possibility even as it mourns the disaster that cancelled it.

Bradman, as it happened came earlier, fractionally earlier, to the Test scene; not with a bang, however, but a whimper. He was part of that defeat at Brisbane by 675 runs, and the scared selectors, observing that he had got his feet in a muddle playing Jack White, rewarded him with the twelfth-man's duties for the next match. His reaction was cool, characteristic, unmistakeable. When he was reinstated for the third Test he made 79 and 112; in the fourth, 40 and 58; in the last and victorious one, 123 and 37 not out. He would have been clear and away at the top of the Australian Test averages for the series, a full 12 points ahead of Ryder and Woodfull, but for his late-arriving friend Jackson, who, appearing in the last two games only, collected 164 in the first Test innings he ever played and finished with an average of 69, leading Bradman by just over 2 points. It is no wonder that the English public, watching with interest as the 1930 series loomed nearer on their doorsteps, had these two young batsmen very clearly in their sights.

And it is the season of 1930 that was chiefly instrumental in piling up, as a direct result of the realization of all English apprehensions, the aggressive incentives which, when the time came round, impelled them to the tactics that triggered the major crisis, the subject of this book. England, the four-to-one victors in 1928-9, were already, unknown to themselves, on a kind of suppressed defensive even before the Australian tour of England in 1930 began; and it was not many weeks before they knew very well that, whether they liked it or not, the defensive was what they were on. Bradman began the tour at Worcester in a manner that over the subsequent years was to harden into a ritual, by making over 200 with barely a chance: to impress observers that this was but a preliminary he scored 185 not out in the next match at Leicester, and over and above such inconsiderable trifles as 78, 66, 44 not out he collected another double century against Surrey and 191 against Hampshire – enough, one would think, for some men for a season and for many for a lifetime, but this batsman amassed these scores before the end of May, holding Nature itself at bay on the very last day of the month and somehow persuading the rain to postpone its arrival until he had scored his 1001st run, upon which play was instantly flooded out. It is no wonder, then, that considerable apprehension developed in home circles, particularly as the controlled aggression of this young man's batting was reinforced by powerful and solid displays from Woodfull, certain menacing auxiliary work by Kippax and Ponsford and very specifically by the most dangerous of the bowlers, Clarrie Grimmett, who even at this early stage had taken all ten Yorkshire wickets in one innings, seven for 46 against Leicester, six for 57 against Lancashire and fourteen for 95 in the two innings of the Hampshire match. The four-to-one victors knew by now in their hearts that the coming Tests were not going to be picnic parties.

They were not: but it is sufficient to remind ourselves that the triumphant English had the Ashes snatched back, not by the odd four runs or the odd four wickets, but by unmistakeably considerable margins. It was not an unusually dry summer, and at least two of the Tests were badly interfered with by the weather; but this did not prevent Australia from compiling several gigantic totals, including 729, 695 and 566, and although it would not be true to say that Bradman made all of these, there were many long periods when it looked as if that was what he was doing. (Those three totals above amount to an aggregate of 1990; Bradman's share was 820.) He failed in the first innings of the first game of the series, and a careful though not very characteristic century in the second innings was regarded as normal and reasonable, something budgeted for, nothing to be surprised at, particularly as it failed to carry the side to victory. And if, even taking into account a hundred by Bradman and ten wickets by Grimmett (not to mention 17 runs as the sum total of the four completed innings of Hammond and Woolley) England could still beat Australia, then perhaps fears were, if not groundless, at least exaggerated. "The suspicion that the England team was riddled with holes" remark Messrs. Barker and Rosenwater, cool and knowledgeable recorders of England-Australia Test history, "was somewhat allayed by this victory."

The illusory contentment had a fortnight in which to savour itself. At Lord's, before His Majesty King George V, (whose arrival to greet the players interrupted a Woodfull-Ponsford partnership of 162 which was broken by the first delivery after resumption) Bradman revealed the power and extent of his genius. In two hours and forty minutes he made 155 without the ghost of a suspicion of a chance; next day he added all but 100, again without fault. It is on record that he and other trustworthy judges beside think this score of 254 to be the most masterly of all his great innings: in intent and perfection of execution it was flawless, and it established him without any manner of doubt as the greatest batsman then playing. And as if this were not enough, having seen to it this time that it was his efforts that had primarily gained Australia the victory at Lord's, he came chirpily in to bat in the second over of the next Test at Leeds and converted the staid face of Test cricket into a kind of benevolent personal massacre, scoring 100 before lunch, 309 by the end of the day, and a record tally of 334 before the Fates had mercy on England. By now the home country were all too clearly aware of their present incapacity to do anything about this newly-arisen terror; so that even an unusual failure in the fourth Test, when he was strangely baffled by the newly-introduced googly bowler Ian Peebles and was out for 14, could not redress the balance, or the imbalance, into anything like its old position. No surprise, therefore, when in the last game of the series, at the Oval (the deciding game, since the third and fourth had been drawn), he went in when a superb foundation-laying partnership by Woodfull and

Ponsford had hoisted the score to 159 and remained at the wicket for two days, fair weather and foul, completing with his devastating 232 a record total for the series (974) that beat Hammond's standing record of 905 by the length of a normal batsman's handsome innings and signed the successful series and season off in his name. It is those few weeks of pre-Test and Test innings that stamped Bradman firmly and finally in the minds of his opponents and colleagues as a quite unprecedented force. Predictable enough, yes: but what was the use when he was apparently impregnable too? The disintegrating England team (who by any other standards had performed with skill, endurance, and a certain amount of individual success) recognised the menace but had precious little idea how it should be countered. He had all the strokes, was lightning of foot and eye, had an ice-cool temperament and boundless stamina; was, to crown all, ruthless, ambitious, successful. Without him, Australia were a fine side that could perhaps by the exercise of traditional skills be contained and possibly mastered; with him, no such matter.

But there was, oddly, just one thing. It was reassuring to realise that he was not perfect, and the realisation, in face of all those double and treble hundreds, took a bit of doing; but there _were_ vulnerabilities, and nobody will honour him the less for that. There was that odd half-hour or so at Old Trafford when the newcomer Peebles cut him very surprisingly down to size: the wicket was deadened by rain and responded well to adventurous spin, and Bradman, who never throughout his great career seemed at home on hostile wickets, was clean beaten first ball as well as missed at slip a few overs later before another snick ended his distresses. This was heartening for his opponents and for those who looked wryly into the future; but wet wickets and masterly spinners coincide too rarely in Test matches, and the likelihood of that kind of coincidence offering itself often, particularly in Bradman's home country, seemed in all conscience remote. His performance against the other bowlers seemed, on the other hand, to yield no hope of any kind whatever. Tate, to be sure, had dismissed him two or three times in Tests, but had paid through the nose in runs per wicket for his pains; Larwood, who had begun the Chapman tour in most destructive vein, had found his penetrative powers diminish surprisingly and dispiritingly thereafter, and had been severely punished as the two series continued without ever getting the great man's wicket at all. Jack White, who had worsted him in his very first game, had been subjected to a very decisive hammering at Lord's and for all Bradman knew or cared had slunk back to Somerset to die. As often as not his wicket went to the honourable stock or change bowlers, Geary or Hammond. In fact it was clear enough that for every problem they were likely to pose he had six or seven answers.

Yet there was, oddly, just one thing, and it did not relate to the Peebles incidents, either. The fifth Test at the Oval, designed to be played to a finish should the rubber depend on its result, (which it did), began in bright warm August sunshine which flooded the field for the first two prolific days. England, after a wobble or two, built what in the pre-Bradman era would have been accepted as a commendably handsome first innings total of 405 and were all out just before lunch on the second day, the Monday. Woodfull and

Ponsford then provided Australia with a very propitious start, Ponsford in particular playing a glorious attacking innings of 110 while suffering acute discomfort from stomach-pains, (inspiring terrifying conjecturings among his opponents as to how many he might have made had be been perfectly fit) and the first wicket did not fall until just after tea. By this time the sun had gone in and the London atmosphere was dimmer than it should be, and Bradman had perforce to play himself in through distracting broken periods while the players went on and off the field for bad light; next morning (Tuesday) the threat of rain was always about, and during the day heavy showers broke up the concentration of batsmen and bowlers alike. Not that they stopped the flow of Bradman's runs, or materially disturbed his successive partners; and at the fall of the third wicket late on the Tuesday morning, he was joined in the middle by that friend and colleague of his of whom we seem to have temporarily lost sight, Archie Jackson.

Jackson had had a rather disappointing tour. There could be no doubt of his class, he was precise and graceful in his movements with a free flow in his style that Alan Kippax alone of his contemporaries could match, but early failures had jolted his confidence and he had not found a place in all the Tests. (When he did play, at Leeds, he was out in the second over, which let Bradman in — see above.) Nevertheless, his failures were not so humiliating as to ruin his self-assurance completely or to obscure his very evident master-quality; and a century against Somerset just before the last Test began helped to secure his inclusion, the robust Victor Richardson, who had not done himself justice in the series, making way for him. In he came, at any rate, at number five, with the score at 263 for three; and proceeded to build with Bradman the longest stand of the innings. He did not get out until Australia had comfortably topped the 500.

It was during this stand that the rain came on, and it was the rain and its effects, every bit as much as the various skills of the two batsmen, that were responsible for the trouble. Jackson came in just before lunch on the Tuesday; what with this, that and the other thing, he was not out until just before lunch on the Wednesday. Ironically, this stand, upon which so much turned, and in a curious way still turns, very nearly did not happen at all; for Jackson, nervous no doubt and anxious to get off the mark after sitting with his pads on for the Lord knows how long, was inspired to play the ball slowly towards cover in the first over he faced and to dash off for what I can only call a hysterical short single. Cover was Jack Hobbs, and to run short singles to Jack Hobbs was never a cardinal tactic prescribed for young Australia or young anyone else at their mother's knee, and the survival of young Master Jackson on this occasion can only be attributed to the sad fact that Jack Hobbs was old enough to be his father. As it was it was a perilously near thing, Hobbs was at it in a flash, but the underarm flick that he fired in at the bowler's wicket was something under a foot wide of its target. Had he hit it, Jackson would have been run out for 0 — he was coming in strongly, but he was yards out still. I was there, I saw it and I know. Jack Hobbs, I can see him still, threw up his hands and covered his eyes in self-chastising shame. Jackson breathed again, and, as I said, was out about twenty-four hours later.

The fine sustaining warmth of the first two days was lost in a reassertion of characteristic English summer weather. Squally showers drove the players on and off the field, wearing three sweaters each. Two substantial chunks were cut out of Tuesday afternoon's sessions; both were the result of rain, and the second in particular was annoyingly prolonged by the persistent refusal of the light to improve. Oddly, it lifted and cleared during what would anyhow have been the last half-hour of the day's play: and the umpires pronounced conditions to be fit for play just in time, if you can believe it, for one over, before the clock struck at 6.30. The Australian batsmen were mildly disgruntled at having to pad up and go out there for six balls only, and no doubt the fielders didn't care for it either; but they went out for that over, and Larwood bowled it.

Jack Fingleton, author of the most succinct and comprehensive account that we have of the Body-line tour and its historical beginnings, put his finger on that one over as the *fons et origo malis*. He had had close contact with all of the players concerned and he may have been absolutely right about this. I have had no comparable contacts, and it is very late in time to re-open the subject now with any prospect of conviction; but I was there and Fingleton was not, and I myself recollect nothing that would substantiate his contention that *this over* was the crucial one. He said that in that over Larwood bowled bouncers at both batsmen, that Jackson was unconcerned when the ball bumped and that Bradman, to put it simply, was not.

I myself would have shifted the bumper incidents to the following morning, and only dare to question the certainty of such an authority because he made such a dramatic point of it. The truth is that the squalls freshened up the wicket, and the effects did not die out readily. When Bradman and Jackson came to bat on the Wednesday morning, (and a dull grey day it was, with barely a fleeting glimpse of the sunlight until the late afternoon) the bowlers found that there was a touch more nip in the wicket than they had noticed at all earlier stages of the game, and Larwood and Tate were very properly eager and willing to exploit it. And it is my clear recollection that Bradman and Jackson, during the two hours on Wednesday morning, had far more short quick stuff on the body to cope with than ever could have been compactly contained in the one over bowled on Tuesday night. What seems to have struck many people at the time, as it certainly struck all the commentators later as they recollected in tranquillity for cash down the transient emotions of the several passing instants, was that Bradman faltered before Larwood's short-pitched deliveries but that Jackson, standing upright and positioning himself firmly behind the line, did not.

Speaking as one, who, like many others who advance opinions on this kind of bowling, would run distractedly backwards towards the square-leg umpire if any fast bowler bumped one at me, I am not condemning Bradman for this, because first of all it is not precisely clear whether the journalist originally responsible for describing Bradman's reaction as "faltering" may at that stage have misinterpreted the extraordinary quickness of this man's reflexes. It is not at all settled in my mind that any of Bradman's reactions to the short-pitched fast stuff were involuntary. His "faltering" may have been a coolly-planned tactical technique. Yours or mine would be a hasty reflex action; he would have had time to organize his. Furthermore, in pointing any contrast between Bradman and Jackson in this contect I am not seeking to draw any sternly moral conclusions. Jackson was taller than Bradman, for one thing; Bradman's instinctive quickness of foot could improvise more skilfully than a less gifted, more orthodox performer. Later in the narrative an examination of Bradman's technique in face of the Body-line attack may show up more distinctly the difference in these early stages between one batsman and another. Nevertheless it seems clear that Jackson met the unexpected bumpers coolly with orthodox methods and that Bradman's reaction was sufficiently unlike his accustomed commanding technique as to set up strange excitements in his opponents' minds. He may not have been as unsettled as he looked; but he was certainly not so settled as Jackson looked − and this was enough to implant in the minds of desperate opponents who feared him to be infallible the notion that he had a weakness.

Whether all that followed would have had the chance to take place if the week of the Oval Test had been consistently fine, who can say? It is good historic showmanship to pinpoint the solitary over on the Tuesday night, or the hour or two before lunch on the Wednesday morning as the magic moment at which and from which the terror emerged − a sort of Sarajevo in miniature. If Jack Hobbs' throw had hit the wicket, would the history of the great game have been altogether different? If Duckworth had caught Bradman earlier, as he ought to have done but didn't ..... the useless conjecturings multiply as you watch. The match itself and the result of it are of less importance than this crucial passage in it: more rain came of course, England were caught on a sticky, and a hopeless second-innings task was made impossible.

A last look at Jackson. He made 73 and was at all times overshadowed; he showed, disappointingly, only traces of his native fluency and charm, and his innings was, said *Wisden* reprovingly, hardly worthy of his reputation. It is clear now that he was never himself during the tour, and that although he was not yet twenty-one the bright skills of his early grace and promise were already being clouded and inhibited from within. The tuberculosis that sapped and destroyed him before he was 24 must have been working in him even at this early stage. Back in Australia he played spasmodically for a season or two, appeared in a few Tests, made several big scores — then illness overcame him and he was lost for good. As one who watched his innings, I can only say that I am glad to have seen him bat and bat courageously; and if, as *Wisden* says, his innings was not worthy of his reputation, this is partly explained by the undisputed fact that that reputation was a mighty high one. In this last glimpse that England ever had of a potentially great batsman, I am sure that not even Sir Donald himself would grudge him the compliment that the chief fact that is remembered about this innings of nearly fifty years ago is that Bradman was disturbed by the attack but that Jackson was not. And it may be that even Jack Hobbs, as the years passed, was glad that his throw went wide.

That noticeable difference between the reactions of the two batsmen did not escape the England captain, Bob Wyatt.

This shrewd and knowledgeable cricketer had, to the accompaniment of a mild sensation, replaced the cheerful and random Chapman as captain for the last Test in what turned out to be a vain attempt to insure for success by substituting solidity for flair. Wyatt himself performed admirably, but at that stage most causes would have been hopeless, and so was this one. Nevertheless, he was quick to spot that disturbance in Bradman's equanimity; he held it in his memory; and in due time he passed it on to his successor as England captain. And it is that successor who now moves to the centre of the stage.

2

JARDINE

Douglas Jardine was, in the context of English cricket, an unusual character; he possessed a certain kind of individuality for which the progress of the game's history had not perhaps prepared either his colleagues or the cricketing public. In a sport which had in its first fifty or sixty years of national repute been dominated almost exclusively by amateurs, and very largely the privileged caste at that, with values enthusiastically absorbed from prep-school, public school, University, regiment and West-end club, Jardine stands very conspicuously as a completely and predictably orthodox specimen who yet contrived to develop into a somewhat unpredictably disconcerting and individualist personality.

Or was it unpredictable? Perhaps not, if it can be agreed that the particular inflexibilities in his character which aggravated, if they did not actually initiate, the crisis under review were traditionally patrician ones. And although it is sometimes misleading to draw ready conclusions from a man's nationality, the fact that he had Scottish forbears must certainly have added more that a touch of pride and perhaps obstinacy to an already quite formidable collaboration of qualities.

His cricket lineage and early cricket beginnings were

conspicuous in their distinction; his father had made a
century for Oxford in a University match in the early 1890's,
and he himself had flourished under early expert coaching at
a preparatory school before revealing himself at Winchester
to be an unusually mature schoolboy cricketer impressive
even more in his orderly and commanding style and grace
than in the inordinate space that all his innings took up in the
score books. At Oxford he took 96 not out off Armstrong's
destroying Australians, (who were trying most of the time);
he eased himself unobtrusively thereafter into county cricket,
into a Surrey side chock-full of accomplished batsmen of
Test class; and during the twenties perfected his classic
techniques into a prolific effectiveness against all kinds of
bowling. Tall, upright, cool, he had the poise that few outside
the circle of the greatest command; he had, whether he used
them or not, all the strokes; he had the rapid reflexes that
availed him on the sticky wickets as readily as his instinctive
free aggressions availed him on the dry. If he had been able to
play regularly, I cannot envisage his omission from any
England side of the late twenties, compact as they were of
some of the most prolific batting artists in the game's history
— Hobbs, Sutcliffe, Hammond, Woolley, Hendren, the list
goes on, but I still cannot see it possible seriously to leave
him out. On his comparatively rare appearances in 1927 he
got 1000 runs in 14 innings; in the next year he got over
1100 in 17. He went on Chapman's tour of 1928-29 almost
as a matter of course, led off with three hundreds in a row
and collected six in all, finishing up top of the tour averages,
if you momentarily ignore Wally Hammond whose figures of
91.35 were 27 points ahead of the field. It must be assumed

that his enforced business commitments, which removed him
from the scene altogether in 1929 and for most of 1930,
effectively ruled out his chances of getting the England
captaincy earlier than he did. Chapman, in spite of his
popular success in Australia, was regrettably losing any
consistency that he may ever have commanded as a batsman;
there is even some mystery in the existing records as to
whether he was absent from the last Test on his victorious
tour through illness or through plain lack of form; he played
little in 1929, and was not available for England in any case.
Rightly, I think, he was persevered with in 1930; and
wrongly, I think, he was discarded for the Oval Test. Wyatt, a
comparative newcomer to Test cricket, was of course the
substitute; but it can hardly be in doubt that Jardine, had he
been available at the time, would have been offered the job at
the Oval.

     But in the next year, 1931, he was back and in form; he
again topped the thousand in only 17 completed innings, in
what was in the memories of all the faithful the filthiest
summer for a generation; and for the first time he captained
his country in a Test — three Tests actually, against New
Zealand, then a somewhat lesser power than they are now. It
was not an exacting trial and only one of the games was a real
contest — weather and sad batting failures vitiated the others.
Jardine himself nothing common did nor mean but nothing
of any moment either, there was not the opportunity. There
was, however, an odd comment by the Editor of the next
year's *Wisden* in his editorial notes, in which he concerned
himself judiciously with the question of the forthcoming tour
of Australia. "It would be idle to suggest", said he, "that the

undertaking is being approached with great confidence."
(You can see what has happened: the Bradman phenomenon
of 1930 has rocked the English cricket establishment to the
foundations.) He goes on a little gloomily through the list of
possibles, tossing around 18 names (of which only 8 were in
the eventual list), and turning finally to the question of the
captain. "Jardine showed last year," he said, "that he has lost
none of his qualities as an exceptionally sound and watchful
batsman: on the other hand he does not seem to have
impressed people with his ability as a leader on the field."

It should be remembered in his defence here, if he needs
a defence, that he had up to this time had very little
experience of captaincy in the first-class game at all. He had
not been captain of the Oxford XI; he had never, except for
an occasional deputising job, captained a county side. In
1931, when he was appointed to lead his country in the three
minor Tests, he was naturally the automatic choice to captain
the Gentlemen in the three matches that were staged against
the Players in that year. Not very many opportunities to
acquire an adequate expertise, particularly when more than
one of these matches was so seriously interfered with by rain
as to render it meaningless in the sight of selectors. The
editor of *Wisden* may have been right, but any judgment
implied in his comment has wilted in the glare of history. Not
only was Jardine appointed captain of Surrey at the
beginning of 1932 but he got the England captaincy against
India – it was their first series and they were allotted one
Test only, at Lord's. This England managed to win, but by no
means easily; in both innings the early batsmen, (who
included Sutcliffe, Woolley and Hammond, and might have

been expected to make the match safe at the outset,) failed alarmingly, and in both innings it was Jardine's courage, skill and resilience that righted the instability and stood as the prime cause of the ultimate victory. These two classic innings, 79 and 85 not out, in their several ways decisive matchwinners both, must have established beyond any possible doubt in the minds of the selectors that here was a treasure beyond expectation. The opinions of the editor of *Wisden* about the quality of his captaincy were losing their relevance already, if they ever had any.

Jardine during these years preceding the fateful tour was one of the most consistently reliable batsmen in the country. The spotlight fastening upon his captaincy, as after the winter of 1932 it was bound to do, has diverted attention from the undeniable fact that he was not only a very good batsman – he was not far off being a great one. I myself a year later saw him play an innings of 59 in the Gentlemen and Players match at Lord's, on a wicket so ravaged by rain and subsequent sun that a highly accomplished batting side was shattered by it, that I rate as the most brilliantly resourceful display I have ever seen in my life of effective artistry under impossible conditions. There is no escaping it: he was at times not just a good, but a great player: and he was confirmed in this not only by the accomplishment of an ordered and finished technique, (which betrayed perhaps a human fallibility against leg-spin) an assured command of all the strokes and an elegant grace in the execution of them, but by as tough and masterful a temperament as any cricketer was ever blessed or cursed with. This had been tried and refined in the exacting Test series of Chapman's tour, where it was notable that certain of his most valuable contributions were built up in partnership with Hammond, in which the latter was by no means the dominant influence: all evidence indicates that Jardine's controlled circumspection imparted to his instinctively aggressive colleague a discipline on which the enormous success both of that series and of his later career was founded. Nor should we forget that during the classic century partnership of Hobbs and Sutcliffe on the hideous Melbourne sticky, Jack Hobbs sent the famous message back to his captain from the middle: "if a wicket falls, don't send in Hammond, send in Jardine." And make no mistake: he was not offering him for sacrifice as an expendable nightwatchman, but as a reliable successor to the masters now in operation. And the sequel was, it will be recalled, that in the fulness of the hours Hobbs did get out, and Jardine did go in, and duly performed the duty assigned to him.

This man was tall, slim, elegant: he moved easily with the disdainful grace of the privileged; he surveyed the surroundings narrowly, out of watchful appraising eyes, his high cheekbones and aquiline Roman nose giving him the air of the exacting Puritanism of Scotland and the rigid stoicism of Republican Rome alike. Those who knew him well, and countless others who played with him and under him, unite in testifying to his charm, his warmth, his loyalty, his reliability. The last two qualities are certainly not in doubt: but those not privileged to be close to him were perhaps not very lavishly treated to the former two. He carried around with him and proffered to his public an air of aloof withdrawal, a mildly Coriolanian distaste for the many-headed. His native aristocracy of feature helped to intensify this; and instinctively or inadvertently he contrived to accentuate this detachment by his identification over the years with the odd symbol of the Harlequin cap.

This characteristic emblem needs a word in these late days to explain it: as in those times it did not. It was, perhaps, even in his period a bit of a survival; but this is not to detract from the distinction that permitted its wearer to sport it at all, and the very proper pride that he was entitled to enjoy in the honour. Broadly speaking it is the prerogative of Oxford Blues only, plus a very few others whom the current University captain has the right to decorate with it; it is conspicuous by its vivid and arresting quarterings of blue, maroon and buff; and it was, right up to the twenties and thirties, worn frequently by old Blues when they played for their counties. In the days before the England cap and sweater were regulation uniform when England took the field, it did not always seem out of place in Tests. Before the first War Plum Warner had assimilated it into his own image; the impression remains that after a certain period no one saw him on the field without it. County cricket was bright with it in the twenties; but I think that Jardine was alone, after that, in wearing it on the fields of highest honour. He is credited with 'invariably' wearing it; this is inaccurate, as I have myself seen him in both Surrey and England colours, and there are photographs of the body-line tour itself which contradict the easy generalisation: nevertheless he sported it constantly, proudly and with a kind of implicit defiance which in a sense, epitomised for those who were opposed to him, a characteristic pride − not to say insolence. The

Australians, temperamentally unacquainted with the local tradition of *charisma* with which it could legitimately be associated in England, instinctively resented it, I think; and it may be that it added marginally to the rifts of mis-understanding and distrust that were presently to appear. There were suggestions that have a way of persisting or recurring, that he cherished a general dislike of Australians — not of particular individuals so much as of a way of behaviour to which he could not warm; and again his most casual action, or even personal idiosyncracy or habit, ran into danger of being interpreted as a deliberate defiance in the teeth of opponents upon whose destruction he was bent. This may have been an unwarrantable diagnosis; but it is an indication of the readiness with which the attitude of a highly intelligent and purposeful man of that particular kind could be hastily but dangerously misinterpreted. It was perhaps unfortunate that the situation was so conveniently set for a confrontation — the spectacular arrival of Bradman so dramatically despoiling England of their recently reassured sense of control, and the natural impulse to avenge this disconcerting injustice embodied now in the personality of a cool and relentless fighter with no very sympathetic feelings towards those whom he was preparing to fight. There are indications that in the period between the Tests of 1930 and the start of the fateful tour of 1932-33 he had been bending his mind to the problem with some care and concentration; a traditional amateur of the old school into whose tem-perament had been firmly and toughly woven certain disconcerting strands of a new and ruthless professionalism.

3

LARWOOD

It had been a long time since English Test sides had relied for their spearhead attack upon genuinely fast bowlers: never since the days of Richardson and Lockwood at the turn of the century had sheer speed been the formula, in spite of the trials that were given to a wide selection of fast opening bowlers of proved merit. The overwhelming success of Barnes and Foster before 1914 accentuated the greater potentialities of the more variously-skilled medium-pacers, who combined, as few really fast bowlers can even hope to do, a bewildering mastery of length, late swing and even in certain cases finger-spin: and these two, though they never could be duplicated, were followed in the early twenties, when real pace bowlers of quality were scarce except in Australia, by the energy and aggression of Johnny Douglas and later the natural and sometimes unplayable genius of Maurice Tate. But these, unlike the conspicuously destructive Australian attackers Gregory and McDonald, never commanded, or attempted to command, the kind of speed which would of itself be a major aggressive weapon. It was this kind of speed that Jardine was looking for in pursuit of the careful tactic which he was slowly and ominously formulating.

By far the best of the genuine fast bowlers to emerge

into English first-class cricket in the twenties had of course been Harold Larwood. The son of a Nottinghamshire miner, he became at an unreasonably early age a Nottinghamshire miner himself; luckily for us and for himself his bowling talent was spotted early, and he was yanked up into the sunlight and on to Trent Bridge at eighteen at the apparently acceptable emolument of thirty-two shillings a week. Within two years he was second in the county bowling averages: within three he was playing for England.

The very sight of his approach to the crease quickened the pulses. He moved so lightly and diffidently, cut such a modest unassuming figure as he took his place in the field, that the energy and power generated in his run-up and action came as an unnerving surprise. Without having seen them all, no one man can discriminate between great fast bowlers; but what fast bowler in the memory of living mortal had a delivery like this man's? He was stocky and wiry and presented a neat compact figure topped off by a shock of fair hair, and he walked quietly and meditatively back for about twenty yards before turning into his notable run-up. I call it notable because it had a quiet concentration about it that I have never seen matched; after the first yard or two it took on the quality of a purposeful and menacing sprint, con- trolled, contained, rhythmical, with a deadly mounting acceleration over the whole distance. (I cannot begin to guess what it must have felt like to be the batsman at whom this manoeuvre was directed; it is a great relief not to have been in the class of proficiency which would have made the experience necessary.) As he reached the wicket he climbed into a glorious whirling poise in which both arms circled at

full stretch above his head and his run was hardly checked:
then at the high climax of this exhilarating performance he
released upon the batsman an offering of thunder and greased
lightning. Other great fast bowlers have had other methods of
attack — Gregory bounded joyously at his victims, McDonald's
devastating bullets were loosed out of the deceptions of a
light caressing grace, Constantine leaped and grinned, Tyson
lunged and lumbered, the list and the variety are in-
exhaustible, and Larwood somehow had a compact
perfection of combined grace and utility that outdid them
all. He demonstrated a classical beauty of movement at the
same time as he embodied an entirely effective co-ordination
of strength and power. There was a direct and purposeful
tenseness about his very expression that was the signal not
only of his intentions but of the superb co-ordination of his
whole body and mind. The wonderful revelation of glory and
strength concealed cool-headed deliberation as much as it
revealed the discipline and precision of the craft of a great
bowler.

This is to describe him at his greatest; not unnaturally he
took some little time to develop stamina and his physique
thus far, to say nothing of his technical capacities — bowling
not being just getting rid of the ball quick, but embodying in
its varieties possibly the subtlest arts that even this subtlest of
all ball games can present for the young cricketer to master.
His arrival among the top players was startling enough,
ramming home to the selectors at once what was at this time
his most conspicuous single attribute, his vicious penetrative
power while the shine was on the ball. Chosen for a Test Trial
at Lord's early in 1926, he opened the bowling for the Rest

against a very strong England side, and proceeded to fire out
Holmes, Woolley and Carr (who made 23 between them) in
the first innings, and Hobbs and Carr (17 between them) in
the second. This no doubt impressed itself rather particularly
and personally on his own county captain, who happened
also to be leading England that season: and sure enough,
Larwood found himself in the Test side for the second game
at Lord's in three weeks' time. This time he was not given the
new ball, Tate and Root sharing the privilege, and his
performance rang no bells; but he was an inspired recall for
the last (and famous) Test at the Oval, and in this contest of
enduring glamour and renown in which not a single England
player failed to contribute *something*, even a small something, to the total of glory, Larwood whipped out Bardsley
and Andrews in the first innings, Woodfull and Macartney in
the second, devastating early blows which were worth in
demoralization value three times the number of actual
wickets taken.

For Notts he was fortunate in being handled by a wary
and intelligent captain who never asked too much of him. His
Test and representative skippers were inclined to overbowl
him; Carr built his confidence and experience up by judicious
stages, bowling him for short spells only and containing his
destructive energy within manageable bounds. Thus he did
not run to the vast bagfuls of seasonal wickets that so many
of the stock bowlers gathered in in those days, but collected
his hundred or so with easy regularity, at very small cost.

Arthur Carr's discriminating treatment of his great fast
bowler was made a good deal easier by the good fortune
which provided his county with another considerable fast

bowler to balance him at the other end. This was Bill Voce, yet another product of the colliery, a formidably tall left-hander who began his first-class career in his late 'teens by bowling slow but was persuaded after a season or two to switch to fast-medium with immediate success. Immensely strong, with a fine high action, he bowled round the wicket with a tireless aggressive persistence, swinging it either way and providing sometimes an even more pressing menace to the batsman's rib-cage than even his faster partner could achieve. There were hints, as he moved into the early stages of his maturity, that he relished bowling short of a length rather more than was comfortable or even seemly; and there is no doubt either that when Voce was on his day Carr switched fielders to the onside more than the orthodox patterns of the game at that time were accustomed to dictate.

Larwood in these earlier days used leg-theory very little; and in his first full Test series against Australia, the Chapman tour of 1928-9, it was the exception and not the rule. He ran into form in his second match on that tour (having been belted by South Australia very comprehensively in the first, none for 116 off twenty overs), and destroyed the powerful Victoria side on a wicket freshened by light rain. This was a mere prelude, however, to a remarkable burst of ferocity in the first Test, when he swept out Woodfull, Ponsford, and Kelleway for nine runs at the outset of the home side's first attempt, finishing the innings off with 6 for 32 in fifteen overs. As he also took four catches in the match and made 70 and 37, he can be said to have earned his passage on that match alone.

This high success faltered in mid-tour; it had been

achieved entirely on the orthodox off-side field, the customary formation with three or four slips and a backward point, with the ball attacking the middle and off stumps, with seemly and seasonable variations. Chapman in the ring of slip-fielders picked up one or two blinding catches, but for the most part these wickets were clean bowled or leg-before. Had he continued the series in the same high strain, his name would have been as perennially linked with its triumphs as Hammond's; but the sting went out of his attack when the tour was half over, and the figures with which he ended it did not reflect his value — not many bowlers' did, it was predominantly a batsman's year. And it may have been at the prompting of some sense of frustration, dissatisfaction, put what label you like to it, that in the fourth Test he tried a little leg-theory. Whether it was his own idea or was suggested by Chapman his captain is not clear; but the account he gives of it himself does not hint that he felt very sanguine about its prospects.

"When I used leg theory in the Adelaide Test against Jackson and Bradman," he says, "I had five or six men on the leg. I bowled rising balls on the leg stump. It was a desperation move to dislodge the batsmen who were on top in hot and exhausting conditions. They both seemed to play it well enough."

Which does not sound very promising, and which paid, as the records confirm, no dividends; in that match Larwood took, in the two innings, one wicket for 152. The experience cannot have left him with any great sense of urgency, little note was taken of it at the time and orthodoxy continued to rule the tactical practises of captains and bowlers. A number

of bowlers who had concentrated their attack on the leg
stump for years and make a living out of it — the most
conspicuous at the time being Fred Root of Worcestershire,
who played for England on the strength of his quick-medium
inswingers delivered to a packed legside field — continued to
exploit this technique with no conspicuous success; and there
are no hints at this time that any of the really fast bowlers
attempted it. The fastest of those who made anything of a
practise of it were Clark of Northants and now, getting a
little nearer home, the menacing Bill Voce, who after making
his place in the Notts side secure was growing taller and
wider, bowling faster and faster, pitching them on the average
shorter and shorter, and packing his leg-side contingent
tighter and tighter. Such success as he did attain in this way
was not so conspicuous as it might have been, since he
continued to mix his techniques and bowl slow as often as he
bowled fast — to the strong satisfaction of *Wisden*, which had
for the last two years been deploring his renunciation of spin
in favour of pace; but when he *did* bowl fast the danger
inherent in this form of attack was taken note of, particularly
from as far away as Australia; and when Woodfull's team
came here in 1930 it was the menace of Voce, not the
menace of Larwood, that privately engaged their interest.
Certain of them conferred before the Notts match to make as
sure as possible that such spearhead as he might be felt to
constitute should be snapped off short, or at least blunted;
Bradman was not playing, but in a high-scoring draw the
tourists made 296 and 360 for four: McCabe, Victor
Richardson, Jackson and Kippax all made fifties, sixties,
seventies, eighties and nineties, Larwood bowled very little (it

was the match before a Test); and Voce, though he did get four wickets in the first innings, took one for 112 in the second and as far as representative cricket was concerned was not seen that season.

No tides flowed very favourably for Larwood in that season either. He was successful enough for his county, to be sure, whenever he could play: but he was unlucky with injury and illness, and missed two Tests, one for reasons of health and one, I regret to say, for reasons of form. At Leeds, the occasion of Bradman's 334, Larwood took one for 139; his confident assertion that Bradman was caught at the wicket off his bowling before he had scored does not seem on examination to be confirmed by the records. At the Oval he did marginally better, taking one for 132, and that one Bradman for 232, whose almost automatic psychological parry was a statement that he did not believe that he had hit the ball off which he was given out caught at the wicket. Larwood's Test record was four for 292, an experience that he was no doubt glad not to have to remember too often.

But for all that, his resilience was complete; he shook himself so free of any inhibition engendered by this failure that in the next two seasons he actually headed the first-class bowling averages, a remarkable and consistent feat by a fast bowler in two wet years. In the first of them he bagged 129 victims, but in the second, the season immediately preceding the tour, he had 162, a very considerable haul for a bowler of his pace who of necessity had to be husbanded. It is clear that by now his technique had been perfected and refined through intensive experiment and practice, that this beautifully vigorous and economically-controlled action was not only producing exceptional speed, but also, what was even more decisive, exceptional accuracy. It is this speed, combined with this unerring control of length and direction, all effected with a kind of purposeful precision, that raised this compact Notts miner in these seasons to the level of a kind of genius dowered with superb gifts and abilities, the chief of which was his power to be able to control them all precisely as he willed it.

4

THE TOUR

Early in August 1932 the touring team was announced, and it cannot be denied that in the perspective it causes the appreciative mouth to water a little as the names pass before the reminiscent eyes. They had better be set out here in column form as they presented themselves to the public in that long-lost month — a promise and a prospect for the winter to come, a stirring reminder to English cricket-lovers that there was a determination in the air to restore, and restore quickly, that balance so lately and rudely overset. Here they were:

> D.R. Jardine (captain)
> R.E.S. Wyatt
> K.S. Duleepsinhji
> G.O. Allen
> F.R. Brown
> R.W.V. Robins
> The Nawab of Pataudi
> Sutcliffe
> Hammond
> Tate
> Larwood
> Verity
> Ames

Leyland

Duckworth

Voce

What a roll-call: no Hobbs admittedly, no Woolley, no Hendren, but no lack either not of class players merely but of men who either had made or were soon to make reputations not just of good but of great performers. The discerning eye can pick from that list at the very least three batsmen in the very highest possible class, with plausible claims for admission to it by two or three more: three great bowlers also, and as far as all-rounders (a catagory drained today of all but the fewest and most select) I can count seven at a blink and I would think it possible to suggest even more. Add to that two of the best wicket-keepers in the game's history, one of whom still remains the best wicket-keeper-batsman ever paraded in international cricket or anywhere else, and head it by a captain of the calibre already outlined, and consider whether any touring team from England, save possibly Warner's supreme 1911-12 force, could face it without beginning to shrivel.

Alas, almost at the very moment of announcement, the fair face of high promise had to be shadowed by dis-appointment. Hardly more than a week after the constitution of the party had been thrown open to all and sundry to appraise and pick to pieces, Nature began its deadly work by eliminating Duleepsinhji, a delightful batsman in the full flow of a free scoring season. Paying as always too much regard to the injunctions of an uncle whose domination over his nephew strikes the dispassionate observer as being unwar-rantably and stupidly dictatorial, he went on playing for

Sussex (who were in full cry for the Championship) when he was clearly unwell; the night after a lovely innings of 90 against Somerset his overtired system rebelled and broke, and although he happily survived a dangerous collapse he never played first-class cricket again. And at about the same time, though without the attendant element of physical distress and danger, business commitments put the reluctant veto on Robins.

Disappointed but resigned, the selectors cast about for replacements. In place of Robins, an all-rounder of brilliant individuality, they settled for a specialist leg-spinner, Tommy Mitchell of Derbyshire, who had been unobtrusively busy among the wickets for several seasons; and although they could hardly replace Duleep they did at least use imagination in choosing his substitute, the exhilarating Eddie Paynter, that model of unpredictable unorthodoxy dressed up as neat conformity. But not even then can the selectors have been sleeping easily; for five days before the team were due to sail, Bill Bowes, who had been ploughing through all Yorkshire's opponents and anyone else's whom he might encounter that season with ever-increasing success in the shape of large numbers of wickets for small numbers of runs, was suddenly prised out of the Champion County match (in which he had just taken the wickets of seven of the best batsmen in England out of eight that had fallen) and told to hurry back to Yorkshire and pack, for he was wanted on voyage. Nor was the situation permitted to stabilise itself; for the intervening five days had not elapsed before Maurice Tate (who had been the last of Bill Bowes' seven, bowled for none, and whether this set up some chain reaction who is to know?) suffered a minor but temporarily incapacitating nervous collapse, which prevented him from sailing with the main party and which may have had disproportionate effects not on Tate himself but on the constitution of the side as it built itself up in the early stages in Australia. He recovered rapidly and followed them out by a later boat; not in time, however, to take any very important place in any Test side, ideal or real, which was by that time forming in the captain's brain.

Bill Bowes had at this moment arrived at the end of a highly rewarding season in which he had considerably extended his reputation and caught the eye of the discerning as well as of the popular Press. The former saw a tall rangy figure whose easy run-up and casual action masked not only unsettling speed but masterly control of swing and lift; the latter saw a promising focus for sensation and concentrated with fervour upon his increasing propensity to drop them short. This tactic was, disconcertingly, not the reflex spasm of an unthinking organism but the carefully-assessed stratagem of a balanced, rather scholarly mind controlled by its intelligence rather than by its emotions; and it seems not beyond probability that this characteristic had in the past few months caught the meditative eye of D.R. Jardine, who had had the opportunity a few weeks before of watching him at twenty-two yards distance at the other end of the Oval pitch. On the occasion in question Bowes took ten Surrey wickets in the match and was the recipient of a public tick-off in front of a large crowd by Jack Hobbs, who objected to having bumpers bowled at his head and walked down the wicket and said so. This seems to have disturbed the bowler very little, (particularly as according to his own account the confrontation was more friendly than it looked from afar) and he finished the season in supremely destructive form, collecting 40 wickets in his last half-dozen matches; and the combination of speed, menace and success very clearly acted upon the susceptibilities of the selectors, who cannot have remained uninfluenced by what must by now have developed in Jardine into a firmly and carefully articulated purpose. At any rate, Jardine, with a formidable quartet of aggressive fast bowlers established centrally in his side, set sail for Australia on 17 September with his mind bent upon vengeance. It did not appear then, nor did it appear later on the tour, nor does it appear now, that he worried much whether Tate, the greatest fast-medium bowler of his generation and still far from spent, was likely to be available or not. The kind of schemes that he was contemplating did not take Tate's brand of genius into account.

But before we watch them down river, one odd occurrence should be noted. When Bowes bowled at Jack Hobbs' head and was spoken to sharpish, there was present in the Press box Plum Warner, one of the most illustrious elder statesmen of the game then living and active in its counsels, and currently cricket correspondent of the *Morning Post*. Not only that, either: he was chairman of selectors, too, and the only one of the triumvirate (the others were T.A. Higson and Percy Perrin) who had ever had personal experience of Test cricket. Furthermore, he had already been constituted manager of the touring side, with R.C.N. Palairet, secretary of the county club on whose ground Bowes was creating alarm and despondency, as his assistant. And Plum Warner delivered himself in the *Morning Post* of an angry attack on Bowes and his bowling methods. "Yorkshire" he said "will find themselves a very unpopular side if there is a repetition of Saturday's play. Moreover, these things lead to reprisals, and when they begin goodness knows where they will end .... On Saturday Yorkshire fell from her pedestal and her great reputation was tarnished .... Once again I appeal to all who control Yorkshire cricket to see that things are altered." And a week later in the *Cricketer*, which he edited, he wrote, "Bowes should alter his tactics. He bowled with five men on the on-side and sent down several very short-pitched balls which frequently bounced head-high and more. That is not bowling. Indeed it is not cricket."

It is of interest to note that one of the batsmen who was subjected by Bowes and later by George Macaulay to a taste of this aggression was the Surrey captain Jardine. There is no record that he protested, or indeed did anything but duck coolly. Furthermore, there is clear record that Bowes did not get him out. It is also of interest to remind ourselves that the cricket correspondent of the *Morning Post* and the editor of the *Cricketer* did not manage to persuade the chairman of the Selection Committee in a few weeks' time not to invite Bill Bowes to make the trip, and I am sure that when he presented himself with his bags and baggage the manager was friendly in his welcome. I do not know whether any reservations were made behind the scenes: perhaps not. It is interesting to remember, however, that this protest was made when it was, and by whom.

Reservations or not, they sailed, as they were wont to then before the days of long distance air travel that can transplant a man from Lord's to the Sydney Cricket Ground in something like thirty-six hours. In those days it was a four-week voyage, diversified by a stop at Colombo for a sort of cricket match; it enabled the cricketers to reabsorb the energies that a tough season and the tensions of selection and embarkation had drained out of them. An Australian journalist, R.W.E. Wilmot, meeting them at Colombo, gave in his book about the tour a mildly scarifying account of their shipboard activities (which need not detain us now, ranging as they did from deck-tennis to male voice choir practice, even including the singing of hymns) and he rounded it off as follows:— "It had been interesting to watch the team spirit developing, to note the confidence the rank and file reposed in the captain. He had not seen much of them, but he was their leader, and he believed in remaining as such. He has the military idea that the general must hold aloof, and he considers that any undue mixing with his rank and file is not conducive to discipline."

Oh dear. So that was what it was like, was it? It is better to withhold comment until we can survey the results of his policies of leadership and pass a more considered judgment on them. It is fairer to follow Mr. Wilmot to his next sentence, which says "In those days on the ship, however, was born the resolve for strong endeavour, that keen determination which in the end was to bring the side through triumphant with the Ashes regained, the credit of England on the cricket field restored."

It is an Australian who speaks, and I must suppose he meant what he said. If the captain were not around to play deck-quoits or sing "Onward, Christian Soldiers" with his rank and file it must be supposed that their confidence in him was being developed by some kind of remote control. This is not the way that Gilligan or Chapman had won the loyalty of their troops; and later in time there was at least one illustrious English touring captain whose team's failure has been in large part attributed to just this kind of aloofness which is here defended in Jardine. As against this, it cannot be denied that Jardine and his memory have attracted, and still attract, remarkably consistent assertions of admiration and loyalty from all those who went with him on this voyage; it is clear that his complex character not only communicated authority but invited respect and perhaps even more than respect. There must have been something altogether unusual about his personality, a compelling singleness of purpose that could dispense with easy charms and graces and yet never fail to call out the responses that he needed. All diagnoses of successful leaders, in whatever field they are active, must take account of this elusive quality. It defies common sense, you would think, but is a successful defiance. Jardine seems to have possessed it.

For the writer attempting to set the preliminary matches of Jardine's tour into normal perspective, there is an unexpected diversion at the very outset. It is the custom, or I suppose it would be more accurate to say it was then the custom, for the first few matches to be played in a spotlight of mounting publicity, and for each member of the side to have his individual performances sifted and assessed in such a high-pitched buzz of artificially-generated excitement as to leave, it would seem, comparatively little energy left for concentration upon the Tests when they were at last attained. The difference about this present tour was this: that there was indeed some frenetic publicity, as was generally expected: but that it was focussed far less upon the personalities and performances of the tourists than it was upon Bradman. I called this an unexpected diversion, but perhaps I was wrong; diversion of one kind or another from the traditional tenor of the game's conduct and the game's conventions was always to be expected when Bradman was about. He was not disruptive, far from it; he behaved himself for the whole of his cricketing career with a decorous and exemplary composure, and nobody ever played the *prima donna* with less overt *panache*. The one thing to be sure of abou't Bradman was that, always within the bounds of ordered and controlled behaviour, he attracted publicity as a lighthouse attracts moths; and on this occasion he was in the thick of it. It is by no means inappropriate that Jardine's tour should begin with this man the centre of all interest. The main theme, though we did not know it, was sounded in the opening phrases.

The enormous success of Bradman's batting on the English tour of 1930 had shot him to stardom overnight; as a result of which he had been guilty of a technical misdemeanour in selling his life story to a newspaper in contravention of a contractual agreement not to write for the Press during the tour. The Board of Control, who at this distance appear to have had right on their side in their condemnation of his action, had in consequence docked him a proportion of his bonus. Bradman took exception to this; and the delicate balance of his relationship with the Board was further disturbed when he applied for permission (as he

was entitled to do) to write on the coming Test series in
Australia while still being allowed to take part in it as a
player. The Board, never renowned for the delicacy of its
diplomatic methods, turned his request down; underlining
their point by granting such permission to Jack Fingleton,
who was a full-time professional journalist and had a stronger
case for acceptance. As a result Bradman threatened to
withdraw from Test cricket altogether; and as a result of that
the Board of Control found themselves at the centre of a
national *brouhaha* beside which the worst excesses of the
French Revolution looked like Sunday tea-time in the Old
Folks' Home. The rights and wrongs do not warrant a
discussion now; but the great Australian public and the 'great
Australian Press made very ugly noises at the prospect of
venturing upon the forthcoming Test struggles without the
greatest Australian batsmen of all time, and several weeks
were consumed in high argument and lost temper before
certain diplomatic counsels prevailed and the matter was
amicably settled. Bradman was released from a contract that
was already held to bind him — on what terms is not known
— and a sigh of relief went over Australia that on still nights
could be heard in England.

I would guess that this blaze of controversial publicity
played the devil with Bradman's nerves. Never mind whether
it was his fault or not: put thewhole thing down to the
unusual complex of circumstances, the emergence of a
national idol at a time when national proficiencies were once
more to be tested, and the threat to that idol resulting from
the operation of commercial and publicity pressures.
Bradman himself cannot possibly have been unaffected by

this. As a cricketer he always seemed entirely unmoved by the customary tremors suffered by the rank and file, and part of his enormous success seems to have been founded on a cool and contained temperamental self-sufficiency denied to all but the highest and the fewest. On the other hand he was not immune from recurrent health problems, of comparatively minor importance usually, but more than once enough to lay him aside for a time; as often as not, I would conjecture, these bouts of indisposition, whatever form they took, resulted from or were aggravated by acute or prolonged nervous strain. And this particular time was, as will be clear enough by now, one when all the possible pressures were on him. It therefore followed that the M.C.C.'s first match after they had landed in Australia, when by tradition they opened their tour against Western Australia at Perth, attracted nothing like the enthusiastic multitudes that poured into the same ground for their second fixture a few days later when a Combined Australian Eleven were marshalled to face them and Bradman was among those listed. The aforesaid enthusiasm had, things being as they were, been whipped up to a lethal state of high tension by the ever-accelerating sequence of contradictions in Press announcements signifying whether the great man was or was not going to appear. First he was and then he wasn't; finally he made good his promise, attracted the eager millions, fielded for two days while the Englishmen made 583 for seven, and did not come in to bat until the third morning after an unfortunate night's downpour had made the wicket ready for Verity. He was then put out twice in one day for 3 and 10, and nobody in Australia even Bradman I imagine, quite knew where to look.

In the first innings he was for once unlucky; Verity was spinning them viciously off the drying wicket, Bradman achieved a thick edge and Hammond took a catch one-handed which would have been no catch at all to anyone else in the side. Such was the opinion of Jack Hobbs in the Press box; who also went on to comment that in the second innings (in which after the first few overs nobody tried very much and a lot of bowling was done by Paynter and Ames) he was not very happy with the pace of Allen. Allen was a fast enough bowler in all conscience, but he bowled no bumpers and employed no leg-side field; it was interesting to note what seemed to be a weakness showing itself so soon. And it is even more interesting to read what Fingleton discloses — that Bradman had told him before the game even started that he was particularly keen to score runs against the Englishmen at this juncture, because he was under the impression that they thought he would be daunted by pace. And in a match in which neither Voce nor Larwood nor Bowes was playing, he quite apparently was so daunted. It is difficult to contemplate Bradman's thoughts, as Pataudi took the catch off Allen that humiliated the national idol for the second time in one day before a capacity crowd of his worshippers, without distress, disquiet, and a certain qualm of sympathy. The limelight can certainly become very hot indeed. It was the beginning, for Bradman, of as difficult and disturbing a passage as his phenomenal career had had as yet to weather. We know that he weathered it, and there is no need for tragic or mock-tragic histrionics: only for a momentary and salutary reminder that in spite of all evidence to the contrary he was a vulnerable human being.

This was at the very end of October, and there was more than a month of necessary build-up before the first Test. There was plenty maturing in Jardine's mind, it is clear; but such public attention as was at liberty to look beyond the immediate crisis that appeared to be forming round Bradman had time to observe that the M.C.C. batsmen for their part were settling into their ordained roles without any delay or difficulty. Sutcliffe began with a fifty and two centuries, Jardine's first three innings included a 98 and a not-out hundred, the Nawab started with 166 and 129 and spoilt it all in his next innings by coming in first wicket down with the score at 223 and being run out for a duck. The others performed sufficiently, flexing their shoulders. Hammond, a thought behind his peers, (if he had any), in striking top form, bided his time until the match against Victoria at Melbourne on 11 November, where they met among the osition for the very first time a young left-handed spinner by the name of Fleetwood-Smith, about whom menacing rumours had begun to trouble the equanimity of the touring side. He had lately massacred Queensland almost on his own, and his name was being deliberately bruited about, in the way that Australian publicity has with it, so that English ears might listen and, if possible, despair. Jardine saw this coming and took Hammond into a corner; as a result of which Hammond went out for the kill, made 203 in an upright exposition of some of the greatest straight-driving and offside play in the century's history and battered Fleetwood-Smith to such a state that he was not called upon that season, as everyone had expected that he would be, by the national Selectors. Later in time, he had some measure of satisfying revenge: but that is another story.

As for the bowlers they had all, with one exception, had a work-out. That exception was not Maurice Tate, by the way, who as will be remembered had not sailed with the team but was even now, in a recovered condition, hastening in pursuit of them across the globe. No, the exception was Larwood, who as a result of a slight skinning of his toes in an early match, went very quietly indeed at the start of the tour and did not bowl in the aggregate more than a dozen overs in the first month. It did not stop him making 81 in forty minutes against South Australia, an arresting reminder that as a batsman he was more than just capable, but was in fact a free and aggressive stylist of considerable quality; but it gave chances to the other leading fast bowlers in the party, Voce, Allen and Bowes, to come to terms with Australian conditions and work up a hostile speed. Furthermore, a nasty and unexpected spell of bad weather in Perth offered an unaccustomed sticky wicket to Verity, who took seven wickets on it, and, much encouraged, took eight in the next match at Adelaide without benefit of weather. It looks as if Jardine at this stage had every reason to feel confident about his prospects for the coming crunch, always provided, and this was a preoccupation uppermost in urgency under that Harlequin cap, that Bradman could be contained. The match at Perth must have given his hopes a vivid reinforcement; and soon it would be time to give the main strategic theories full public practice.

In the match at Melbourne already referred to that had featured the planned dismemberment of Fleetwood-Smith, Larwood was not playing; Allen and Voce provided the pace and virtually shared the wickets until the last day, and it was in the course of their entirely successful assault on a rather depleted Victorian team that Voce bowled to a predominantly legside field a form of attack that would later be stigmatized as 'body-line'. Even then he did not stretch its possibilities, planting only four fielders in the ring of menace that was later to establish itself as a sinister symbol: one forward short leg, two short legs behind the wicket and one away in the deep. Whether or not he then bowled short, or appeared as a more urgent threat to the batsman than he had with a normal field does not appear very clearly in accounts of the match. At any rate this first try-out of a new policy attracted little attention at the time. Fast Voce may have been, but he was not as fast as Larwood. The curtain was not due to rise just yet.

Nevertheless it was all ready; Jardine was presumably only waiting until his bowlers and fieldsmen had found themselves on the quicker-paced wickets and until his team was sufficiently co-ordinated as a happy and willing unit before he developed his idea to the scale of a full-size operation. It is now certain that the hints and intimations of which the hindsighted chronicler is only too aware, though he must be chary of affording too much importance to too many *trivia*, must all have been gratefully received by Jardine as the months went by and assembled by him as the basis for his major strategy for the tour. Bob Wyatt had not been slow to pass on his account of the interesting Bradman reaction to the freshening-up of Larwood's speed during the famous short-pitched overs during the Oval Test; he had observed with keen interest the dislocating progress of Bill Bowes around the counties in the summer of 1932 at all distances from twenty yards upwards; and certain rapid liaison-work by Percy Fender had enlisted the co-operation of Arthur Carr, who brought both Larwood and Voce to a close conference round a dinner table at the Piccadilly Hotel during the August Bank Holiday match at the Oval. ("Although it took some time to warm up Larwood and Voce," records Carr sardonically, "to talk in the company of their not exactly hail-fellow-well-met captain-to-be in Australia, they did eventually get going." The picture is engaging and authentic.) This was not all: it was reported then, and later, that he had gone even further back in history and sought out Frank Foster, the brilliant aggressive fast medium left-hander who had been such a worthy and effective partner to the great Barnes on the triumphant tour of 1911-12, using six fielders on the leg and kicking it into the batsmen's ribs. (The story is that Foster offered ready and helpful advice, but in the cold light of dawn, when the battles were over and the smoke had cleared, felt less than happy about the results of it.)

All these stealthy and systematic preparations were the essential technique of a careful campaigner. Jardine's very aloofness contributed to the general feeling that a new strategic intelligence was ticking busily away and would reveal itself in its own good time. It is possible that he consulted his team, or some of them, on the voyage out or during the journeyings in Australia itself (although I have it on the authority of one of the most prominent members that so far as he knew he did not); but he was not a man to wear his heart or his strategy on his sleeve, and when he issued an order or communicated a decision the party of the second part was expected to jump to it and no questions asked. This authoritarian quirk led to more than one unnecessary disagreement — in particular one with Bill Bowes in the early match against South Australia at Adelaide, when the captain without disclosing his reasons refused the bowler an extra fielder on the leg side but offered him five, which he hadn't asked for and didn't want, calming down only after a show-down and a detailed explanation in the cool of the evening: a crisis for which I cannot help feeling the captain was entirely to blame. Full of great enterprise and the hopes and ambitions associated with it, he was perhaps less immune than he should have been to the failings of the single-minded, who have no time or space for the indulgence of the common requirements of their fellows. It is at any rate beyond question that at that time and for the preparatory months before it he had one consuming purpose and his eyes were bright with it. Even while he was yet upon the high seas, the garrulous and enthusiastic Home Gordon, writing an article about him for the *Cricketer Winter Annual*, had reported in a twitter of excitement that Jardine had lunched with him before leaving on the tour and had disclosed to him in confidence a method that he had devised for beating the Australians in the coming series of Tests. Gordon very properly went no further than this, and left all his readers in a pleasurable quiver of anticipation. Whether or not the theory that Jardine disclosed to him then was the one which he put into practice when he got there with his team, nobody now can say. Very probably it was; although it has been cogently argued, by people in a position to know, that the methods ultimately employed evolved from spontaneous impulse rather than from carefully planned theory.

Nevertheless, that theory, enlarged into practice, became what is now called Body-line. This was a term coined for it during the tour by a more or less incensed Australian journalist; Jardine conceived of it rather as Leg-Theory and however euphemistic his severer critics may judge this to be, it was the theory with which he started and it is best to expound it that way. In strictness it had little to do with the intimidating bouncer with which Bill Bowes in particular and nearly all other fast bowlers in general were (and are still) wont to try the skills and more specifically the nerve of the opposing batsmen. Its origins lay in the less aggressive but even more persistent tactics of the medium-paced inswingers concentrating on the line of the leg stump, of whom Fred Root already referred to was perhaps the most successful and the most consistent; but to this mild bottling-up manoeuvre Jardine added not only an alarming intensification of speed but a fearsomely impending cluster of waiting fieldsmen. Where Root had at the most three fielders on the leg side, Larwood was to be accommodated on occasion by as many as seven. Moreover, the necessarily random menace of the bouncer was to be replaced by the factor on which Jardine with his chosen team of practised attackers was most confident that he could rely — persistent and unwavering accuracy of direction. Allowing for the normal coefficients of human imperfection it was going to be a fair certainty that when Larwood or Voce bowled a ball on a certain length and to a certain direction, it had gone where the bowler had intended it to go. The batsman was therefore faced with an attack that varied strikingly (and the word is carefully chosen) from the fast bowler's customary line, which is to direct his speed and swing at or about the off stump with the intention of forcing the batsman to play and snick to a half-circle of waiting slips. Here Jardine had at his command bowlers who were ideally cast to take advantage of the fact that in Australia the conditions of pitch and atmosphere alike cut the normal fast bowlers' outswing to a minimum. Under English conditions Larwood could swing the new ball away from the batsman for five or six overs at least before the shine went off; in Australia this potency barely lasted beyond the second over, and he would normally find from then on that his body-action would naturally bring the ball in from the off and that the direction of nearly all the defensive strokes would be to the on-side. Jardine's concentration on leg-theory was therefore a rational move rather than a sadistic fancy. In England an early mis-hit off a fast bowler would be more likely to go to the off: in Australia, to the leg. It was, in essence, as simple as that. In theory, nobody can blame Jardine for adopting an alternative which was more likely to get the wickets than the other. And here the accuracy must again be insisted upon: inaccurate bowling on the leg is probably more expensive than inaccurate bowling on the off. Jardine could not have ventured on this had he not trusted the quality of his bowlers.

The batsman taking guard against Larwood or Voce, then, was likely to be surrounded by an orthodox field — three slips, backward point, deep third man, short leg, deep fine leg — for the first two or three overs. Once the shine and the swing departed, the ominous switch would take place;

and the batsman, looking round the field before settling down to make what he might of one of the fastest and most accurately hostile bowlers of all time, would be assured of the presence, within a few yards of him as he took up his stance, of Jardine and Sutcliffe in forward short leg positions, Allen short and square just on his tail, Voce and Hammond short and fine over his left shoulder, and Wyatt dropped back on the fence to entrap any injudicious airborne hook. A mid-on or another deep square leg or midwicket would complete the enchainment. As the worried man bent to his bat, and Larwood, far away, began on his glorious run-up, the sense of imminent menace must have mounted like a wave; and he would immediately be confronted with the probability that the ball when it came (and come it would, rather soon) would arrive on the line of the leg stump. If it were pitched on a full or normal length he could normally play it without discomfort; but a ball on the short side delivered on to those Australian wickets, by that particular English bowler or his mate, took the whole transaction out of the region of comfort altogether, particularly as in those regions the angle of bounce was unpredictable. A *very* short-pitched ball might be a Bowes-type bouncer and rocket skywards; this could be judiciously avoided if spotted in time; but a not so very short pitched-ball rearing into the neck or ribs off a length or a point just short of it would present the most brutal of alternatives − (1) play an orthodox defensive shot and risk being caught relatively easily by Jardine, Sutcliffe, Allen, Voce or Hammond (2) hook it hard and risk being caught almost as easily by Wyatt at fine leg or Leyland at deep square leg (3) lie back and cut, or try to, which will result in a spreadeagled wicket if the ball *doesn't* get up (4) interpose the body and take the consequences, which might conceivably be fatal. It is easy here to put oneself in the batsman's place and decide that the alternatives are so unpleasant that the best plan would be to take up tennis; it is also necessary to be fair to the devisers of these alternatives and agree that the tactic is within the law and that the target is *not*, repeat *not*, the batsman's body but the batsman's confidence. There seems to me to be a difference — it may be a subtle one, but I believe it to exist — between the scientific ordering of this kind of leg-side attack and the outspokenly stated attitude and intention of its most conspicuous successors, Messrs. Thomson and Lillee. "I want it to hurt so much," the latter stated, or caused to be stated, in print, "that the batsman does not want to face me any more." It may possibly be argued that it comes to the same thing and that it is not very relevant to argue that what Jardine's policy meant in similar terms was "I want it to confront the batsman with a succession of tactical dilemmas, in each of which physical fear may have a part but not the most important part, or even an essential part." This may be easier to determine as the chronicle unrolls: what is perfectly clear is that, horrendous as Thomson and Lillee could be, in Australia at any rate and no doubt elsewhere when conditions were in their favour, they did not have at their backs the same kind of determined logical policy that Jardine conceived or, I am bold to suggest, the technical accuracy that Larwood commanded, nor did they have the support of a crowded legside field. They were two gifted and vigorous individualists thirsting for blood, honour and glory, and frequently being rewarded with all three at once; Larwood was a highly disciplined athlete operating under detailed orders dictated by a practised and ruthless tactician. Once again I leave the nature and result of any difference between the two sorts of attack to be determined as the tale proceeds.

Three days after the end of the match against Victoria at Melbourne, the tourists were on view again on the same ground, but this time against another combined side, (titled in fact An Australian XI) which included under Woodfull's captaincy a number of highly promising young players, a leavening of more solid experience, — and Bradman. After his double failure under the merciless spotlight in Perth, the great man's feelings, however well concealed under that inscrutable mask, must have been, I feel, of a kind that no-one would wish to share; particularly as he found deployed against him the entire range of hostile fast bowlers in the M.C.C. party; (although, as it turned out, Allen, the only speed bowler to dispense with leg theory altogether, only bowled three overs in the match). It was an odd game in that climate on that wicket with those batsmen: for on an easy pitch the tourists batted tentatively and disappointingly, and were pinned down to a very moderate score for those regions, 282. Hammond was not playing, and nor, as a matter of some interest, was Jardine; but the batting line-up was still formidable and the bowling opposition by no means of intimidating quality. Only Sutcliffe and Paynter performed with much solidity or effect; and the incentive then naturally passed to the fast bowlers.

The first over Larwood bowled was only his twelfth of the tour; and he seemed to have conserved his energies for the effort. He and Bowes, who was given the new ball in preference to Voce or Allen, worked up from the start a very notable pace; and not long after the beginning a ball from Larwood reared off a length and struck Woodfull a capsizing blow over the heart. The Australian captain, one of the most courageous and tenacious players in the game's history, took no time in recovering and resuming, but it was an ominous note to strike, and Bradman must have watched it from the pavilion with feelings of some foreboding. It was Bowes who got the first wicket after Larwood had been temporarily rested, and Bradman came in to play what up till then was perhaps the oddest innings he had ever played in his life. "He played strokes," said Ray Robinson, "as much like a carpet-beater's as a batsman's — what's more, a carpet-beater in a hurry to get through with the job." He swatted at the short bouncers when they came as if he were dismissing flies from his presence; he hustled nervously about the crease on quick uneasy feet, overbalancing once and tickling a single off the edge of a bat waving in the air from an ignominious sitting position. When Larwood came back and planted his five leg-fielders within breathing-distance he countered the fast leg theory either by dodging to square-leg and slashing through gully, if he could, or hopping briskly to the off and letting the ball whistle past behind his back. That he lasted for three-quarters of an hour and made as many as 36 is solely attributable to the fact that he was a great opportunist batsman and that even in these hectic circumstances opportunities occurred, which he took. Nevertheless even his own colleagues were mystified. Some of them even thought, quite seriously, that he was cutting these capers to deceive the

English, who would accordingly bowl short stuff to him in the Tests and get minced for their pains.

This kindly theory spoke much for the deserved esteem in which his enormous skill was held; but it flattered him. I would be very wary indeed before I committed myself to the belief that Bradman was rattled; but I can convince myself that he had been taken by surprise and had not yet been able to construct a successful technique to meet this kind of attack. His reactions may have looked like panic: what they were, in fact, amounted to a series of spontaneous improvisations. How his comparative lack of success affected his confidence it is impossible to guess, but it cannot have reinforced it. More particularly it must have undermined that of his team-mates; the contemplative eye of Woodfull can hardly have lightened at the sight.

This was an odd match; after leading the Australians by 64 runs, almost entirely through the devastation of their middle order by the three fast bowlers, the M.C.C. side collapsed for 60 in a formless rout before a tall fast-medium swinger named Lisle Nagel from Victoria, who took eight for 32 in ten overs and left the game wide open. The Australian side, carrying with it not only Bradman and Woodfull but such other Test batsmen of the present and the future as O'Brien, Rigg, Darling, Oxenham and Ben Barnett, were set a mere 125 to win. There had been rain in the air on the third day when Nagel did his damage — no doubt it had freshened up the wicket and given him an additional lethal nip that destroyed the batsmen with its extra foot or two of pace — and it was imminent on the last day when the final round was engaged. Wyatt this time asked Allen to share the new ball with Larwood.

Rain cut this fearsome passage of arms to seven overs only. Jack Hobbs, observing proceedings from the Press Box and no doubt (even he) preferring to be there rather than opposite Larwood and Allen at this juncture, recorded that the bowling looked "very dangerous stuff" and that he did not think Larwood had ever bowled faster. It was also once again observed that the leg-theory field was set after the first over or so, even though Wyatt was captain and not Jardine, (who, it was reported, was not even present at the match but had awarded himself a quiet few days fishing up-river). Allen,

During these four overs Larwood ran one away from Woodfull, who was snapped up triumphantly by Duckworth off a thick edge; and Bradman on his arrival continued his eccentricities of the previous innings. He was in no way successful with Larwood, who bowled even faster to him than he had to Woodfull, and contained him and his partner O'Brien almost runless. Allen, in spite of his great speed and admirable length, was a slightly easier proposition for him, but even off him the runs he delivered came hurriedly and off the edge; he was not fighting his usual commanding battle, and when he once more faced Larwood in the seventh over of the innings he retreated towards square leg to give himself room for a slashing square cut, found too late that the ball kept lower than he had expected and was clean bowled, stranded without dignity or decorum with 13 to his name. As he turned for the pavilion the crowd lapsed into a shocked silence. It cannot have been happy or easy to have been Bradman at moments of this kind of failure; the weight of renown and responsibility that he was, rightly or wrongly, being made to carry must have made any deviation, from success, however pardonable, exceptionally hard to sustain. The heavens, in sympathy, opened immediately afterwards; and the game virtually ended there.

This game may have made an end, but it was in itself a regrettable beginning, and it is difficult to find fault with the natural reactions which began to show themselves at this time. The Australian players, never mind the spectators for the moment, were naturally waking up to a feeling that the nature of these international contests, whether at Test level or lower, was being injected with an unaccustomed virulence. Aggressiveness was to be expected and nobody minded it, having weapons to counter it with; but what looked far more like planned deliberate intimidation was not in their book, and quite apart from the actual physical difficulty of countering it effectively and the even more imminent physical danger of being dealt a damaging or even a lethal blow, there was an attitude of mind, a kind of cold implacability, implicit in the tactic that they were not prepared for and which they roundly hated. This feeling gave immediate and understandable rise to personal coolness between the players on and off the field; and when home teams and visitors stop having drinks together after the day's play, or reinforce the proper hostility that is implicit in the game's routines with an improper hostility that fosters personal distrusts, then it is time to look to the defences of the game itself which cannot be immune if players cease to respect it. A very eloquent and telling complaint comes from Jack Fingleton, who had a right to lift up his voice if anyone had, because in the next match after the rainy Melbourne struggle he saw more of the new tactics than any one Australian had yet had to endure. The M.C.C. team proceeded to Sydney to play New South Wales, who were swept comprehensively out of the way and beaten by an innings. Larwood was rested, and so was Bowes; and for the first time the tourists had the services of Maurice Tate, who had caught them up at last and who was responsible for cleaning up the first four batsmen with all his old stampeding fire, just as if it were a salty Saturday morning at Hove with the breeze off the Channel and the new ball swinging in the sea-fret. He comes into the broody atmosphere like a reviving wind, taking four for 53 and lifting all hearts while doing so, for he was welcome back and had been missed, and never bowled leg-theory in his life; but he blows out of it as smartly as he blew in, for Jardine's tactical schemes took no account of him and for the rest of the tour he was relegated with George Duckworth and Freddie Brown to the permanent concourse of camp-following accessories, whose functions were largely to give the regulars a rest at Wagga-Wagga.

The damage at the other end in the New South Wales first innings was almost exclusively accomplished by Allen, and if you look at the score-sheet you will wonder at the gloom and despondency with which Fingleton later described his recollections of the game. For this admirable and courageous batsman, who had by then barely put his nose inside the confines of Test cricket, carried his bat staunchly through the collapsing innings, was assisted half-way down by the brilliant Stan McCabe in a fine resourceful partnership of 118, and survived unbeaten at the fall of the last wicket with 119 against his name. Yet he confessed that he felt none of the elation or satisfaction that he would normally have expected to enjoy; all he could be conscious of, he said, was the crash of his youthful ideals. Playing against England in actuality had proved vastly different, he said regretfully, from what boyish dreams and adventure had imagined it to be. The reason in this particular match was probably referable to the deterioration in the atmosphere of normal friendliness that I have already noted; but it must have been partly centred in the only leg-theory practitioner actively operative in this game: Bill Voce.

Voce, said Fingleton, bowled very fast that day and gave as vigorous an exhibition of body-line as any seen in Australia that season. The fact that although he bowled more overs than Allen or Tate he only took one wicket suggests to me that he lacked Larwood's destructive accuracy. Fingleton said quite frankly that he bowled short and he bowled at the body, using sometimes five short legs with two men covering them in the deep. He goes on to say that for all the good the stumps were they might as well have been left in the pavilion; anything that didn't hit the batsman in the ribs cleared the leg stump or (he adds) a space outside the leg stump, by feet. Fingleton condemned this bowling out of hand as malicious and intentional, and I cannot think of anyone who was in a better or more authoritative position to say so than a man who was repeatedly hit by it and yet made 119 not out while it was going on. Voce, with one wicket for 53, may have wondered whether his pains and his consequent unpopularity were justified; but perhaps they were, and it may have been Jardine's pleasure, even if he were not himself successful, to use him as a softener-up for the others.

In the second innings Voce rang the bell much more effectively; after New South Wales had fielded out to an innings of 530 (Sutcliffe made a superb 182, and Wyatt, Ames and Pataudi all made good scores) Voce took five for 85 and nobody played him with confidence, though it would be unfair to withhold commendations from F.S. Cummins, number seven in the order, who made 71 when none of the top-liners got to 30. And talking of top-liners, it must not be overlooked that the flotsam and jetsam once more included Bradman. Tate had trapped him l.b.w. for 18 in that first glorious liberated burst of his in the first innings; and in the second, desperately (or calculatedly?) employing against Voce the extravagant improvisations that he had previously tried with little success against Larwood, he bent his head and shoulders and shuffled towards point in avoidance of a bumper which never bumped but hit his wicket behind his legs. It is not possible to contemplate this series of temporary dislodgements with any pleasure, even if one's sympathies are committed to his opponents: and it is in a sense a relief to be told by certain of the contemporary accounts that, unsurprisingly, he was by this time far from well and, in fact, batted at number 6 in the second innings, coming to bat, says one report, from a sick bed. If excuses are to be sought, here is a sufficient one to hand. He was going through a version of hell at this time, it cannot be gainsaid, and it is common enough knowledge that worse was round the corner; but he weathered it.

The New South Wales game finished on 29 November; and the First Test, on the same ground at Sydney, was scheduled to start on the 2nd of the next month. For their part the English team approached the occasion with some confidence. Leaving aside the manner in which it had been achieved, a formidable captain had united a formidable array of players into a formidable combination, and had ended up very much on top in all their preliminary matches whether they had actually attained to victory or not. Furthermore the batsman whom they feared most had been apparently demoralised; he was still a danger, and the size to which he had been cut down was still a size larger than most Test batsmen could hope to equal; but he had been cut down, and that was something to start with. As I say, we must discount for the moment the manner of this achievement, and we must try to ignore the unhappy coldnesses and snipings that were adding an unpleasant rancour to an otherwise satisfactory atmosphere of progress and hope.

5

FIRST TEST

Let us get the preliminary sensation over at once; on the afternoon before the first Test began Bradman was declared unfit to play. To anyone reading as dispassionately as possible the account of the preliminary matches of the tour this can come as no surprise: the disconcerting instabilities of his public performances reflect many enigmatic and imponderable conflicts, which cannot have failed to include nervous strains operating disastrously upon the player's mental and physical co-ordination. It was wise of him to have succumbed to them when he did; no useful purpose could have been served by his continued public immolation. He withdrew under doctor's orders and took a rest. It is stated, somewhat surprisingly, that, also under medical advice, he then proceeded to spend a fortnight at a seaside holiday camp. I hope he felt the better for it.

Off he went, then, and the remnants prepared to do battle, lining up on the first morning as follows:-

Australia:

W.M. Woodfull, W.H. Ponsford, V.Y. Richardson, A.F. Kippax, S.J. McCabe, J.H. Fingleton, W.A. Oldfield, C.V. Grimmett, T.W. Wall, W.J. O'Reilly, L.E. Nagel.

England:

D.R. Jardine, R.E.S. Wyatt, H. Sutcliffe, W.R. Hammond, Nawab of Pataudi, M. Leyland, L.E.G. Ames, G.O. Allen, H. Larwood, W. Voce, H. Verity.

No great surprises here; Bradman's absence of course cut Australia's batting strength down quite drastically, but a glance along the names reveals prodigious possibilities still. For their effective bowling they would appear to have to rely principally on Grimmett and the dangerous O'Reilly, playing his first Test against England. Wall was a reliable but not devastating opening bowler, while Nagel had been swept in on the crest of his last week's wave of destruction and was as yet inexperienced in these high strata. Ironmonger, whom good judges thought should certainly have played, was left out. The batting suffered from a long and not very flexible tail; which could not be said of the English team, every one of whom at one time or another made a hundred in first class cricket. Ames, who had trailed through Chapman's tour as Duckworth's understudy and had figured then in no Test matches, was introduced now on the strength of his superior skill with the bat, and in fact found himself preferred to Duckworth for all the representative games both on this tour and the next. As for the attack, Jardine did not push speed to the absolute extremity; he left out Bowes, relying principally therefore on three fast bowlers and Verity, with Hammond as principal reinforcement. Characteristically, Jardine did not announce his team until the coin was tossed; he did not even announce it to the seventeen tourists themselves, who were all instructed to change into flannels and wait in the dressing-room until required. He learned his psychology in an odd school.

To his extreme annoyance and despondency, he began by losing the toss; his gloom not relieved by the assurance of one of the Australians who had taken part in the Australian XI game at Melbourne that the English fast bowlers would not be able to get the ball above knee-high in Sydney. Philosophically resigned to letting events take their course, he opened with Larwood and Voce, delighted in due course to find the Australian's judgment disproved, as a ball in Larwood's first over pitched a trifle short of a length and missed Woodfull's head by inches - this to an orthodox offside field. Taking heart from this, no doubt, Voce at the other end bowled leg-theory from the start.

This, not unnaturally, set up reactions in the crowd. Sydney's celebrated 'Hill' did not get its reputation for nothing; and it set the tone not only for this particular match but for the intensified crowd-responses that were to be one of the signal features of the series. "From the time we went on the field" said Larwood, "the crowd used to roar from beginning to end. They would count me out until I delivered the ball, trying to put me off. Cricket spectators today just don't realise what it was like then." (Larwood wrote those words, or caused them to be written, in 1964; since then the increasing crowd-response at Test and Prudential World Cup matches, especially at those involving the West Indies, is perhaps beginning to re-create for modern eyes and ears something of the eruptive atmosphere of those far-off days.) The players in those days had to grow a protective shell of indifference among all this sound and fury, and grow it quick; and all consideration of the Tests on this particular tour has necessarily to be coloured by the realisation that for the greater part of the time the intricate and exquisite familiar patterns were traced out in an atmosphere of screeching mindless pandemonium. Larwood sensibly enough refused to be put off, even when the whole mob screamed "Left-right, left-right", in time with his run-up in an endeavour to put him off his length (it presumably having failed to occur to them that this might possibly disturb the concentration of the batsman.) He came to terms with it as far as he could, cocking agreeable snooks at them when they roared and making defiant and unrefined gestures in reply. They bore him no malice for this, it appears, except for the odd fanatics who wrote abusive threatening letters - in fact, one barracker wrote rather apologetically to say that the rowdies were out to do anything possible to help Australia win, that there was nothing personal in it, he would go on doing the same tomorrow but no hard feelings. "It's not you we're up against, it's your ability. Take no notice because you give us what we want — you give us our money's worth." This endearing little piece of naiveté rescues some of the episode from the pits of crowd-hysteria into which the whole prolonged episode threatened to slide, and into which so much of the modern publicity-swollen sport has disastrously collapsed. I hope it was some consolation to the players, as the jungle noises howled about them, to realise that this treatment was only being handed out because they were giving the crowd their money's worth. Whatever incentives lay obscurely behind it, it increased very perceptibly the high degree of tension to which for one reason and another this ominous series was already being screwed.

Before this tension had reached its height, Woodfull had flicked one of Voce's rare away-swingers to Ames, and Bradman's substitute at number three, Jack Fingleton, had set himself sturdily to build with Ponsford a reasonable foundation for an Australian innings. The wicket was playing so straightforwardly as to give the bowlers no help; but

Larwood and Voce, bowling mixed orthodox and leg-theory, and bowling with great speed and accuracy, gave them no opportunity to settle. Fingleton, barely blooded as yet as a Test batsman, found his determination unshaken but his resources of defence tested to full capacity; Ponsford, great and highly prolific batsman with ten years first-class experience behind him, was discovering that the Larwood of 1932 in Australia was yards faster than the Larwood of 1930 in England, and finding it hard to come to terms with his new methods of attack. Shuffling tentatively across his wicket, he was the bare shadow of the batsman who had so mercilessly thrashed Larwood's opening overs at the Oval only two years before; the two held out valiantly until lunch time, when the score was 63, but Jardine must have felt that the prime emphasis of the morning's play had offered clear compensation for the lost luck of the toss.

Almost immediately after the interval Larwood's accuracy and pertinacity, toned up during the morning period and invigorated by the break, broke through the uncertain defences. With only two added, Ponsford shuffled over to the off again, was beaten by an unexpected extra yard of pace and lost his leg stump. Larwood on the kill, it is interesting to note, eschewed the short stuff, pitched on a fuller length, and overcame the defences by his sheer catapulting pace, forcing the batsman to hurry their shots seconds before their inbuilt reactions could operate. Fingleton was snapped up at short-leg; and the free graceful Kippax, compelled to the defensive and deprived of both freedom and grace, was pinned l.b.w. by a good length ball that he had no time to bring his bat to, arriving back in the pavilion with the laconic remark, "He's too bloody fast for me." Three wickets had gone in half a dozen overs and the score was 87 for four; at which point, with Larwood 3 for 20 and not unnaturally losing the first and most penetrating freshness, and Voce with all his insatiable energy and toughness also revealing a tendency to tire, the tide was stemmed by Stan McCabe and Victor Richardson, numbers 5 and 6, conscious of the presence in the far too immediate future of a tail several yards long.

It is this partnership which gave one of the partners the chance to play the innings of a lifetime – or perhaps it would be more accurate to say, one of three great innings that he was to play in Test cricket that sign his own genial immortality and put him among the greatest masters. Stan McCabe may not have been the greatest Australian batsman of all time, but he could easily qualify to be the most attractive – a brilliant quick-footed master of resourceful attacking play, as light and graceful as his shots were powerful and assured. An innings of 189 not out that he played against South Africa in 1935 and a very notable 232 against England at Nottingham in 1938 were each given outstanding praise by Bradman, (and who better qualified to judge?) and together with the one that we are now about to watch him play, are ranked by good judges as the three greatest innings seen on Test fields in the decade before the Second World War. (They have Hammond's 240 at Lord's in 1938 to compete with as well as Hutton's 364 and a whole handful of innings by Bradman; it does not matter, and there are no prizes offered, so long as we realize what class we are in.) Here was McCabe, 22 years old, walking in to face a

leg-theory menace to which nobody had any satisfying reply
ready and which in this very game had already dislodged
three most experienced Test batsmen in an uncomfortable
hustle without presuming to reach intimidating levels: as he
walked in to face Larwood, being wished good luck by his
parents who had come up from the hinterland to watch him,
he said to his father, "If I happen to get hit out there, keep
Mum from jumping the fence."

He and the tall capable old campaigner Victor Richardson
shored up the ruins and introduced stability. They were
perhaps a little fortunate in that the chief reinforcement
called in by Jardine to relieve the tiring openers was Allen,
who not only did not and would not bowl leg-theory (and
later reached an understood compromise with his captain
about this, not without a measuring-up of personalities) but
on this occasion bowled below his best. McCabe and
Richardson, free batsmen by nature but compelled for a time
to shrink into unaccustomed shells, maintained stability and
after a time began to assert something more.

McCabe for the first and possibly the only time in the
series provided the effective answer to leg-theory; he attacked
it. He stepped back to the first short ball that Larwood
bowled him and hit it crisply off the middle of the bat to the
square-leg boundary. It sounds easy; and yet, if you use a
trifle of imagination and remember Larwood's pace, and even
Voce's, you cannot help shuddering at the sober fact that the
fraction of a split second that the speed allowed you to
decide what position to get your feet into in order to play an
attacking shot was a very very small fraction of a split second
indeed, and if you mistimed your shot you stood a fair

chance, if you had positioned your feet correctly, of being hit somewhere vulnerable, and hit paralysingly hard. On this day (and even more so, on the next) McCabe's good fortune abetted his courage and skill. It must be remembered that not everyone would have been well advised to dare what he dared; but his ability was of course such as to warrant the brave attempt. And McCabe was not one, once he had committed himself, to engage upon this kind of adventure half-heartedly. In fact, to sum up, he pasted Larwood, Voce, Allen, Verity and Hammond all over Sydney Cricket Ground: and it was no indiscriminate pasting either, but a careful and systematic attack delayed deliberately until he had played himself circumspectly into a command of the various talents combining to attack him.

In all this we must not forget Victor Richardson. This immensely likeable and talented player seemed at the very last edge of all — unlike nearly all his Australian friends and, of course, relations, which include his formidable Chappell grandsons — to be a brilliant and gifted amateur rather than a dedicated and single-minded professional. Heaven forbid that his qualities or his whole-hearted deployment of them should ever be called in question; but there was a kind of cheerful *insouciance* about his free and courageous batting and his conspicuously adept fielding that left the perhaps quite erroneous impression that he enjoyed the whole thing so much that it would spoil everything for himself and the rest of us if he were to take it as deadly seriously as everyone else seemed inclined to. Again, this may be an illusion; but the impression remains that in the highest reaches he was more inconsistent than the greatest should be, that he carried with

him, as well as an engaging enthusiasm, an even more
engaging vulnerability. But that he was a highly accomplished
batsman no English opponent ever doubted; and on this day
in particular it was as much his resolution and capacity as
McCabe's that rescued Australia from the pit. In face of
Larwood, Voce, Allen and the rest these two hoisted the
score from 87 to 216. Of course they were hit about the
body a bit; but McCabe shrugged it off and Richardson was
constructed of leather and brass. Richardson showed the
way; McCabe took it; and by the time that Richardson was
caught in Voce's leg trap, going for the run that would have
brought him his fifty, McCabe had forced Jardine to relax his
field placing and to switch Larwood back to the old
orthodox ways — against which McCabe's off drives and
square cuts were as effective as his hooking had been when
the leg-theory heat was on.

One more wicket fell that night, but at the end of play
the score was 290 for six. The very considerable improvement over the disastrous 87 for four represented the first
considerable rebuff that Jardine had ever faced since in-
troducing his new tactic; and of the 208 runs that had come
since McCabe said goodbye to his Mum and Dad in the early
afternoon, he had made 127, with nothing as yet in the
semblance of a chance.

Next morning three wickets fell quickly, but not
McCabe's; Voce and Larwood, coming fresh to the attack,
were too quick for the tail-enders, and try as he might
McCabe could not keep them away from the bowling all the
time. But the last batsman, Wall, no more accomplished a
performer than his earlier colleagues, somehow contrived to

stick; he arrived with the score at 305 for nine, and the last pair added 55 in just under that number of minutes, of which Wall, galloping valiantly up and down and taking time off to applaud McCabe as he cut loose and took every risk in the book, made as many as 4. McCabe used all the strokes, and when Larwood shifted to leg-theory he used all that that hampering technique permitted him and was otherwise unperturbed. On the few occasions when Wall had to face the attack he never faltered. It was a brilliant and invigorating stand, it sent the Hill and its environs into a delirium of excitement, and it hoisted McCabe's name, not only for the time being but for ever after, up beside Victor Trumper's. For the moment Bradman's absence was forgotten; and nobody contemplating the history of the last few weeks would have expected him, even if he had come in then and there, to do as well. When McCabe was 170 he cut Larwood viciously to backward point, and Voce (excusably) dropped it. That was his only technical blemish. When at last Hammond got rid of Wall and the innings closed for 360, McCabe came in with 187 not out, made in four hours enlivened with as many as 25 fours, thirteen of which were from the glorious leg-theory-defying hook. It was to prove to be the most exhilarating and life-enhancing innings of a series to which neither of these adjectives seems particulary apt. It is a pity that the high flair, which from time to time could transform McCabe from a fine batsman into a great one, could not have been more constantly at his command in this series. Such heightening of Australian morale as it supplied could perhaps have sweetened the subsequent encounters.

The very formidable English batting combination now

proceeded to move into action. In terms of those days 360 was no very unattainable target, and Sutcliffe and Wyatt were completely unperturbed. The opening attack of Wall and Nagel was steady but no more: the nip coaxed out of the wicket by Larwood and Voce was entirely dormant for the home side, and by the time Grimmett and O'Reilly took over, the defences had been too deeply founded for any serious danger of overthrow. Sutcliffe settled as quietly and firmly as ever − in spite of suggestions that he was instinctively missing his classic opening partner and that the role of Number One was a thought incommodious to the greatest Number Two in cricket history; and Wyatt, himself a kind of Sutcliffe in mould and temperament, was an entirely reliable partner. 112 was up before Grimmett pushed one through and found Wyatt's pads in front; and it can have been little relief to the Australian fielders to find Hammond taking his place.

One piece of good luck had come England's way, and it has solidified in history as a *locus classicus* − Sutcliffe played on when he had made 43 and the bail quivered but failed to fall. While umpires and players clustered excitedly around, Sutcliffe calmly leant on his bat ten yards off, taking the air with a lordly assumption of indifference. Rewarded with a reprieve, he reassumed command, and was still there at the end of the day, 116 not out, Hammond 92 not out. England 252 for one.

Apart from McCabe's *bravura* performance, this was the finest batting of the match: calm and impregnable competence at one end, poised controlled aggression at the other, two great masters at the peak of their mastery, it needs no more detailing than that. Here was no massacre; merely formidable defence founding a long and prolific innings, with Sutcliffe laying the firm basis and Hammond showing the way to the necessary accumulation to follow. Even the experienced and always dangerous Grimmett found them impervious; and O'Reilly, however effectively he was later to disturb these batsmen and their peers, was not able to do more that day than contain them within reasonable compass.

Next morning the tale was for an hour or more the same. The stand overnight had amounted to 140; it got to 188 before Hammond with 112 to his name miscued a drive and was caught, with the total at exactly 300; and the Australians had to endure yet another century partnership between Sutcliffe and Pataudi before any further success accrued. This, although richly prolific of runs, was a slower and perhaps less satisfactory affair, as Pataudi was for the whole duration of a century innings somewhat drearily inhibited. We cannot take away from him the positive credit of a hundred on his first Test appearance, a very happily-rounded completion of a signal sequence of successes by the three great Indian batsmen Ranji, Duleep and Pataudi himself, who had now each celebrated his first innings against Australia by making a hundred; but when you have said that you have said nearly everything. Sutcliffe went at last for 194, his highest Test innings ever; Pataudi stodged on, but somehow the life went out of the remaining English batting. The last five wickets went for 54 and the valiant Australian attack were in a measure rewarded for their persistence by having the lead cut down to as low as 164, the tail (which rather surprisingly included Ames) slithering before O'Reilly in an untidy series

of noughts. At one point the score had been 423 for two; so
a total of 524 had almost the effect of a kind of restored
balance.

Almost, but not quite; for before the Australian second
innings could get itself under way Larwood shot out
Woodfull for nothing, and Ponsford, bowed under the weight
of disaster past, present, and to come, was once more bowled
behind his legs as he huddled forward outside the off-stump,
(Woodfull, with 55 as his aggregate for the six innings he had
now played against the tourists, was in no better fettle than
Bradman; and little that his accredited batsmen could do in
this innings could have given him much confidence.)

McCabe, indeed, promoted a place, faced Larwood this
time with all the sturdy optimism of the first innings, toning
down the brilliance but never abrogating the courage and
resource; and he and Fingleton batted as well as anyone.
Larwood after a slower beginning — he was hampered at first
by a slight strain, which appeared to wear off — began to
work up to his highest speed. Fingleton relied on straight
defence; McCabe lay back and hooked. Jardine for a time
rested his openers and varied the attack with Allen and
Hammond; and it was Hammond, varying his speed and
exploiting a worn patch, who broke through, getting McCabe
l.b.w. and Richardson caught in the slips at the same total,
61. Kippax and Fingleton tried all they knew to stem the
tide; but when Larwood, coming back after a rest, was again
too fast for Kippax, the resistance all but crumbled away;
Larwood in one fierce burst of leg-theory collected four
wickets for 13 runs, and the game looked to be over, and
over in a few minutes.

It was not quite over, though; there was determined and rather effective resistance by Nagel and Wall, the ninth-wicket pair who, when everybody saw that their cause was hopeless and yearned to have done and go home, added 38 brave runs against the cream of the England attack. When Allen got Wall caught at the wicket Australia needed 13 to avoid an innings defeat; and in the closing overs of this fourth day Nagel and O'Reilly actually contrived to make exactly those thirteen and no more — and what is more contrived not to get out; a courageous achievement, a great joke, and a great nuisance; requiring the presence of twenty-two crick-eters with necessary officials, staff and associate flotsam and jetsam to turn up bright and early tomorrow morning, day Five, to play the play out.

And there they were, on the next morning, washed and brushed, with the sun high in the heavens and all to play for. Voce clean bowled O'Reilly with the third ball of the day; everyone trooped off the field and in due time, I suppose, trooped on again for England to score one run. (Whether a new ball was used for the purpose would be interesting to know.) McCabe bowled, Sutcliffe turned it neatly off his pads, they ran one, the spectators cheered, and all was left to the sparrows. England had trounced Australia in the very next match after the heavy Bradman defeats of 1930, her fast bowling technique had overwhelmed a very formidable collection of batsmen with the outstanding exception of McCabe, honourably supported by Richardson and Fingleton, Australian morale was nearly as vitally shattered as English morale in 1974-5 by Lillee and Thomson, and England's batting was for the most part ready for anything that even the most illustrious Australian bowlers could do to unsettle them. As against this, it had to be remembered that Bradman had not been playing; and that the increasing noise about the ears of the fielders indicated less of a joyful and companionable welcome than an increasing and shortly barely controllable resentment. With these debits and these credits, they proceeded towards the next Test via some holiday matches in which Tommy Mitchell got packets of wickets and cheap runs were in plenty.

It was during this Test — which, as will be soon apparent, was by no means as acrimonious as certain of its successors — that the fatal word was coined, and coined apparently almost by mistake. A week or two before the game, the Melbourne weekly *The Australasian* had carried an article by the old Australian Test batsman Jack Worrall, who described the bowling of Larwood and Voce in an earlier match as "half-pitched slingers on the body-line" — no very elegant phrase,but I suppose it may be allowed that it described no very elegant technique. This caught the eye of Hugh Buggy, correspondent of the *Melbourne Herald*, and he, required to telegraph from the Sydney ground in a luncheon interval with a hurried stop-press message, included the following phrase: "Voce was hit for six, again bodyline bowling"; and it should be noted that this was deliberate telegraphese not intended for literal transcription. He was instinctively relying on the Melbourne sub-editor to expand the words for publication into "again bowling on the line of the body." The sub-editor in question, none other than Ray Robinson, later to develop into one of the finest of all Australian cricket writers, jumped at the word "body-line" and sought to use it in a headline. His editor, stepping delicately, said no; but had no objection to its inclusion in the text. It caught on: and in the rather rapid fullness of time went round the world and back, and whether anyone or everyone liked it or not, it was and is there for ever.

The English cricketers in particular found it an objectionable word: to them it carried accusatory and resentful implications that they did not relish and to which they took exception. Larwood calls it a hateful, malevolent word; Jardine, when he heard of Buggy's part in its invention, regarded him, says Larwood, with cold hostility whenever their paths happened to cross. At this distance of time I see it as a descriptive rather than a pejorative term; but I was not there and they were. It has, for better or worse, passed into the common language of this specialized corner of what may be called civilisation.

AUSTRALIA

W.M. Woodfull	c Ames b Voce	7	b Larwood		0
W.H. Ponsford	b Larwood	32	b Voce		2
J.H. Fingleton	c Allen b Larwood	26	c Voce b Larwood		40
A.F. Kippax	lbw b Larwood	8	b Larwood		19
S.J. McCabe	not out	187	lbw b Hammond		32
V.Y. Richardson	c Hammond b Voce	49	c Voce b Hammond		0
W.A. Oldfield	c Ames b Larwood	4	c Leyland b Larwood		1
C.V. Grimmett	c Ames b Voce	19	c Allen b Larwood		5
L.E. Nagel	b Larwood	0	not out		1
W.J. O'Reilly	b Voce	4	b Voce		7
T.W. Wall	c Allen b Hammond	4	c Ames b Allen		20
	b 12 lb 4 nb 4	20	b 12 lb 2 w 1 nb 2		17
Total		360			164

	O	M	R	W	O	M	R	W
Larwood	31	5	96	5	18	4	28	5
Voce	29	4	110	4	17.3	5	54	2
Allen	15	1	65	0	9	5	13	1
Hammond	14.2	0	34	1	15	6	37	2
Verity	13	4	35	0	4	1	15	0

ENGLAND

H. Sutcliffe	lbw b Wall	194	not out	1
R.E.S. Wyatt	lbw b Grimmett	38	not out	0
W.R. Hammond	c Grimmett b Nagel	112		
Nawab of Pataudi	b Nagel	102		
M. Leyland	c Oldfield b Wall	0		
D.R. Jardine	c Oldfield b McCabe	27		
H. Verity	lbw b Wall	2		
G.O. Allen	c & b O'Reilly	19		
L.E.G. Ames	c McCabe b O'Reilly	0		
H. Larwood	lbw b O'Reilly	0		
W. Voce	not out	0		
	b 12 lb 17 nb 6	30		
Total		524	(0 wkts)	1

	O	M	R	W	O	M	R	W
Wall	38	4	104	3				
Nagel	43.4	9	110	2				
O'Reilly	67	32	117	3				
Grimmett	64	22	118	1				
McCabe	15	2	42	1	0.1	0	1	0

England won by ten wickets.

6

SECOND TEST

The English team, heartened by success, spent the rest of the last day at Sydney (which, it will be remembered, had lasted for four balls, one wicket and one run) in strenuous practice, carefully and strategically organised by the captain. Satisfied with their progress so far, they were certainly not going to relax; and Melbourne, their next Test port of call, with its reputation for hard wickets and high scores, was going to need if anything more determination than their first essay at Sydney. Jardine was not the man to play this one easy; and as the day drew near he determined to throw all he had into the contest. Accordingly he brought in Bill Bowes and left out Verity; going into the field with what has since been called the worst-balanced bowling side ever to represent England in a Test, four fast bowlers plus Hammond, with Leyland, who in the end got one wicket on the whole tour, as the only conceivable approach to a spinner.

Laughably enough, Australia's bowling change was in the reverse direction. Nagel, his crowded hour of glorious life now completed, was discarded (as it happened, for ever) and Ironmonger, for whom in the long hours of English batting domination at Sydney the Australians had found themselves craving, was restored to the side. Otherwise the bowling ranks were undisturbed; but in the higher reaches of the batting seismic changes were ordered. The positive gain, of course, was the return of Bradman, now much recovered (and no doubt relieved and happy to be facing Larwood's leg theory after a fortnight at a holiday camp); but as against that was the sad departure not of one but of two hitherto established and highly-honoured Test stars, Ponsford and Kippax. (The indifference of the Australian selectors to the stability and morale of their players may be gauged by the almost unbelievable fact that right up to the very morning of the match Woodfull did not even know that he would be playing, much less captaining the side. This cannot have contributed very conspicuously to the establishment of confidence, whether personal or collective.) Bradman of course took one of the vacant batting places; while the other went to Leo O'Brien, a promising left-hander from Victoria, playing his first Test. Oddly, Bradman made a request at about this time that he be allowed to drop a place in the order of going in, an indication that he was not yet quite the master of his fate that at better times than this he was accustomed to be; and O'Brien was allotted the key position of number three, with the world's greatest Number Three following him in at Number Four. But wherever he batted, Bradman was going to be not merely the centre of attraction but the key to the future of the match, and perhaps even of the series.

Once again Jardine lost the toss; and the game had not been in progress for more than twenty minutes or so before the ball went out of shape, Larwood's boots developed structural troubles and had to be attended to, and to crown Jardine's rising accumulation of annoyances, the famed and feared Melbourne wicket was yards slower than anyone had ever known it to be. (Some Englishmen averred that it had been deliberately over-watered to take the sting out of the England fast attack: whether this accusation was deserved or not, it was the fruit of logical assumption, and the fact remained that the sting *was* taken out of the England fast attackers.) Larwood, apart from a ball or two now and then, could get little real pace out of this docile pitch and both leg-theory and orthodoxy were courted for some time in vain, punctuated by time-wasting visits to the dressing-room for repairs to his boots.

What with this, that and the other administrative delay on account of balls and boots, and the failure of the pitch to yield the expected sparks, a funereal pace was imposed upon the game from the start, and even the head-high bumpers seemed to arrive in slow motion. To add to the general malaise Melbourne sweltered in uncomfortable heat, and Jardine was obliged to use his bowlers in shorter and shorter spells. The still uncertain Woodfull departed at 29, clean bowled by Allen, and at lunch, with the newcomer O'Brien matching Fingleton's dourness with his own very natural sedate watchfulness, the score was only 42. After an hour or so of defensive sparring after the interval, during which 25 more runs were imperceptibly added, a natural impatience overcame O'Brien's reticence and in an understandable attempt to speed up the scoring by snatching a quick single, he was run out; which let in the great man himself, the moment for which the whole vast crowd had consciously or unconsciously been waiting all day.

It was quite usual for him to be greeted with a roar of applause, but nothing like this engulfing welcome had been heard outside anyone's dreams. Bradman walked in slowly, as he always did, to accustom himself to the light, but the cheers accompanied him to the moment he took guard and after, causing Bowes, who was the bowler, to be baulked twice as he attempted to start his run-up. When at last the cheering faded and he began to move in, he saw Bradman moving too, his right foot preparing its straddle across the wicket for the hook off the short bouncer that he felt instinctively was due. Bowes, sensing this, dropped it short but did not dig it in; the dead wicket obliged by its unresponsiveness, the ball reared, but not to its expected height, and although Bradman's quicksilver reactions changed his purpose in mid-stroke, it could not save him, and his abortive hook-shot edged it down into his leg stump. I cannot imagine that in the whole history of first class cricket any single man can have ever had to endure a worse moment of crushing public humiliation than this. The vast crowd received him back among them in an almost unbearable silence.

Ironically, it would appear, the Melbourne wicket had been almost entirely responsible for Bradman's disaster. He had spent much of his holiday working out ways and means of countering the short fast stuff which was clearly to be the staple provision for the series; he had made up his mind to concentrate on two things — dodging the bumpers, and scoring runs, both of which, if he used his brilliantly quick footwork and hooked or slashed to taste, he could guarantee to do. It is surprising that one of his steely level-headed disposition should have been hurried, as he clearly was, into this conspicuous error, whose effect was so disproportionately dramatic. His temperament had clearly not quite recovered its necessary poise. The shock still disturbs, more than forty years later. I am a lifelong England supporter, who suffered untold misery for twenty years from Bradman's overwhelming mastery; nothing pleased better than a rare Bradman failure. Yet somehow, given all the circumstances, this one leaves no sense of triumph or satisfaction behind it; for once he is human, a sufferer, one of us.

McCabe came in to do what he could, and with Fingleton anchored sturdily at the other end did his best to repeat his Sydney aggression. He brought a fluency and grace to the game that it had not yet seen; while Fingleton's tough courage began to earn him runs as well as a growing confidence. The partnership put on 64 before McCabe's natural ambitions betrayed him into an uppish slash, and 25 runs later Fingleton, who through canny and watchful intelligence was beginning to look like a circumspect master of the leg-theory attack, was beaten and bowled by Allen, the one fast bowler who did not use it. Richardson underpinned the incipient collapse with his own brand of defiance, but at the end of the dour and unsatisfactory day Australia had lost seven wickets and were still short of the 200 mark. Oldfield refused to be cowed in the morning, but Larwood found little resistance in the rest of the tail, and 228 (*with* Bradman this time) seemed so modest a target that English morale must have been of the highest when the opening pair went out to bat.

It was not long before this was dispersed, and with no mistake about it. The Australian batting had been courageous but unresourceful, confronted with a menace they had not mastered and uncertain of their tactics. The English with no such terrors to overcome, faced an accurate and increasingly relentless attack with no confidence at all. Even Sutcliffe the imperturbable, who got to fifty, had to be imperturbable about an alarmingly high tally of catches dropped off him; nobody played with conviction, no England batsman can look back upon the innings, which tailed on all day for a miserable 161 for nine, with any pleasure or satisfaction. These were in fact the very legitimate perquisites of Wall and O'Reilly, both of whom bowled with intelligence and thrust on a wicket that showed signs of wear when it showed any signs at all. O'Reilly in particular with five wickets for only 63 off 34 overs declared himself then and there and once for all as probably the most dangerous and potentially devastating of the Australian bowlers; Wall's four wickets were Sutcliffe, Hammond, Jardine and Ames (what a four!), for 52 runs only; and Grimmett applied a further crippling brake by bowling 16 overs for 21 runs. This half-hearted display surprised England supporters and surprised the England players themselves; dark looks and comments were directed at the wicket, which may or may not have been responsible for the wholesale failure of a very notable list of batsmen but which beyond doubt had upset the sanguine calculations of both sides and turned the match into a series of major and minor disappointments, individual and collective.

Next day England were soon all out, 59 behind, which in the context of that niggardly match was a considerable deficit. Part of this was neutralised at once, for Allen, brought early into the attack when Larwood asked to change ends, caused Fingleton to spar instantly at an outswinger, and

Ames accepted the snick. Woodfull and O'Brien did their best
for as long as they could, which was not very long, to shield
Bradman from the opening furies: but the score was only 27
when Larwood, now switched to the other end from that at
which he had started the bowling, beat O'Brien by sheer
brute pace and knocked his off stump out of the ground in a
series of exhilarating cartwheels. Which, of necessity, brought
in Bradman.

It would perhaps be too much of an exaggeration to say
that any other contemporary batsman in the position in
which Bradman found himself at this moment would have
felt that he was facing his last chance, but the tensions
inevitably active within him as he approached the wicket now
must have approximated to those attendant upon a major
crisis. To go in facing the prospect of a pair, wherever you are
and whoever you are, is bound to intensify all normal
nervous reactions to the point of trauma; to go in at the
climax of a long-drawn-out crisis of more than two months'
standing and to know that you are the focal point of an
unprecedented nation-wide adulation, that an innumerable
and insensate public has entrusted you with an almost
unbearable emotional responsibility, and to remember that
your last seven innings against this crucial opposition have
been failures — can the sympathetic imagination do more at
the moment than bow and retire? These thoughts, or others
like them, were quite sufficient, no doubt, to engage his mind
as he walked in at 27 for two to replace O'Brien and
rehabilitate himself as best he could. And the bowler now
waiting to bowl to him was Larwood.

The ensuing few hours without any doubt produced the

finest cricket of the match. For this we have of course to thank the high skills of the batsmen, bowlers, fieldsmen and strategic cricket brains concerned; but especially we have to thank this strangely uncharacteristic Melbourne wicket, which deadened the life and fire and took much of the lethal sting out of Jardine's planned shock tactics. How often during the course of this game he must have devoutly cursed his relegation of Verity and the comparative ineffectiveness of Bowes is a matter for sardonic conjecture only; for apart from the one celebrated success Bowes found no inspiration or venom and could provide little of his own; and in this second innings when battle was joined in thrilling earnest it was Hammond whom the captain relied oftener upon as telling variant, and Bowes only bowled four overs. With leg theory if not innocuous, at least blunted for the time, the shock bowlers had to rely on more orthodox expertise, and Larwood in particular bowled with superb accuracy and speed. Nevertheless Bradman, and secondarily the admirable Woodfull, played with a cool settled competence that defied for a time all the visionary demons that the previous history of the tour had called into existence.

Bradman and Woodfull saw away the lunch interval far less jumpily than of late, playing shots crisply, scoring with more freedom than their recent tentativeness had been able to achieve. It was a hot day and the fast bowlers tired quickly, having to be shuttled in short spells. (Larwood in particular was in trouble with his boots and with his temper, relieving the latter with some short-pitched stuff, the forerunner of events to come). The powerful Hammond was of high value as auxiliary, bowling tight medium pace, giving little away. Balance was once more established; once more it was suddenly overset when Allen caught Woodfull at short leg off Larwood, and an over or two later, to the immense satisfaction of the English, clean bowled the dangerous McCabe for a duck.

Australia were 81 for four, and at any time the innings could have toppled and come down in ruins; a wicket here or there, particularly Bradman's wicket, could have undermined the whole precarious structure. But Victor Richardson was an admirable colleague in a crisis, and the Bradman now in charge was ominously solid as well as ominously productive of runs — not the old impregnable and irresistable plunderer yet, but clearly a master and more evidently so with every over. It is interesting to note that in the stand with Richardson it was the impregnability rather than the irresistibility that prevailed — they added 54 together and Richardson's share was 32, a most uncharacteristic division of the spoils — but everyone in Australia from Woodfull downwards must have welcomed this enormous access of responsibility. It is also pertinent to look ahead and observe that when Richardson was out at 135 five wickets remained to fall; in the end the total came to 191; and of those additional 56 runs only nine came off the bat of anyone but Bradman. It was Hammond, rather than Larwood or Voce, who trapped and troubled the tail; in an extremely tight spell of ten overs, the great majority of which in the nature of things was delivered at the best batsman in the world, he took three for 21, and Jardine says frankly that he does not know what he would have done without him. Relied presumably upon Larwood, Voce and Allen, already bowling

their hearts out, and the unfortunately ineffectual Bowes. At
no time did the shock bowlers abate their accuracy; at no
time, in this innings, was Bradman shaken from his firm and
masterful poise. The later batsmen came, played their
secondary parts as best they might, and departed; Bradman,
farming the bowling carefully, urging his partners to quick
runs, watchful in defence and murderous towards anything
loose, took control of the scoring. He hit 9 off one of
Larwood's overs (unprecedented this trip) and temporarily
spiked his guns. When Ironmonger came in at number eleven,
reputedly one of the worst batsmen ever to play Test cricket,
Voce and Hammond were sharing the bowling and Bradman
was 98 not out. To the intense delight of the crowd
Ironmonger lasted out Hammond's over, and Bradman
topped up the tension by playing all but the last ball of
Voce's next straight back to him. Then with the last ball
came release — Voce pitched it short and Bradman hooked it
for four, and the subsequent explosion could be heard on the
other side of the world. An over or so later he ran
Ironmonger out in an attempt to keep the bowling; but he
had achieved a personal and a public redemption and made
for himself a monument more lasting than bronze — well,
perhaps not that, but it must have seemed like it at the time.

"Bradman's glorious innings" said Arthur Mailey, "stood
out from those of his team-mates like a diamond set in pieces
of glass." This from a writer cast in the impish and whimsical
rather than in the appreciatively lyrical mould is a genuine
and warming tribute to a welcome assertion of quality. Even
Jardine, well down in the list of Bradman's admirers, could
scarce forbear to cheer. "By far his best and most worthy

innings of the series .... he obtained the complete mastery which so many Australians associate with his batting ..... at the top of his form, playing a great innings for his side." Praise from Sir Hubert is praise indeed.

The close of the innings at 191 left England with 251 to get to win; the highest total of the match, on a wicket already suspect and prone to unpredictable variations of height and pace. Bradman had weathered this against pace: Australia's attack would include one pace man it is true, but three major spinners, who on a fourth day and a wearing wicket would be no picnic. For all that, 251 was a target accessible enough for healthy hopes; and Jardine with perhaps some underlying faith in the superior efficacy of Yorkshire doggedness, altered his batting order and sent in Leyland with Sutcliffe to see the last hour through.

Bravely they did it; Wall was not kept on long and the main attack was sustained by O'Reilly and Ironmonger, coming in low and exploiting the spinners' wicket. Sutcliffe's uncertainty of the first innings was now all gone, and at this fearsomely responsible stage he batted like the controlled master he was. At the close of play they had made 43; and the more sanguine of us English, absorbing at our breakfast-time radio sets the encouraging news, retailed less directly and competently than nowadays but retailed all the same, went to our day's work with heightened hopes. Sutcliffe was there still, so was Leyland. Leyland was not Hobbs, a pity, but he was Leyland, a splendid asset. 43 for no wicket could not have been bettered as an encouragement for the last run-in.

Ten minutes on the next hot bright morning sufficed to

wipe the grin off English faces; after Leyland, opening with crisp confidence, had taken nine quick runs off the first two overs, Sutcliffe was beaten and bowled by O'Reilly with a superb ball moving from a length on the middle and leg stumps to flick the top of the off. Leyland without addition swung across a fast long-hop on his legs, the ball kept disconcertingly low and bowled him off his pads; and Hammond was all but bowled with the last ball of Wall's same over. This drove England very naturally on to the defensive; and it took Hammond and Pataudi nearly an hour to grind out the next 18 runs, after which Pataudi's inconclusive dab off Ironmonger was picked up in the slips and Jardine came in to receive three balls all of which beat him by the spin, the last fatally. Then at 77 Ames, who with Hammond seemed to have decided to try to hit these bowlers off their length and had entered upon a determined campaign of aggression accordingly, was splendidly caught by Fingleton at deep square leg, and Hammond, who had scored most of the runs since Sutcliffe's departure and was now adventuring sturdily off the front foot at every opportunity, was caught off one of his long hanging drives at deep extra-cover at 85. Now only Wyatt and Allen, as accredited batsmen, stood between England and the deep sea.

Wyatt and Allen were England's last chance and they batted for nearly two hours with gritted teeth. As the noonday wore on into the afternoon the wicket eased a little, its vagaries were subdued, the batsmen played more confidently, the admirable partnership clocked up its 50. 135 for 6, 116 to win; given fortune, skill, endurance, it was not an impossible task and for a short space a fluttering hope was once again revived. But no, on the whole things don't happen like that, and they didn't then: Wyatt was out l.b.w. (the eighth time since landing in Australia), Allen was brilliantly stumped two runs later, and the rest was formality. They didn't get 116; they got 4. O'Reilly with five for 66 brought his tally to ten wickets in the match, Ironmonger with four for 26 in 19 overs showed up the complete indispensability of spin, and the Australian crowd, chairing their champions into the pavilion and howling their heads off in legitimate delight, saw off a finely-contested game to its entirely justified result. The English at their radio-sets back home had disappointment to mix with their breakfasts that January morning.

AUSTRALIA

J.H. Fingleton	b Allen	83	c Ames b Allen		1
W.M. Woodfull	b Allen	10	c Allen b Larwood		26
L.P. O'Brien	run out	10	b Larwood		11
D.G. Bradman	b Bowes	0	not out		103
S.J. McCabe	c Jardine b Voce	32	b Allen		0
V.Y. Richardson	c Hammond b Voce	34	lbw b Hammond		32
W.A. Oldfield	not out	27	b Voce		6
C.V. Grimmett	c Sutcliffe b Voce	2	b Voce		0
T.W. Wall	run out	1	lbw b Hammond		3
W.J. O'Reilly	b Larwood	15	c Ames b Hammond		0
H. Ironmonger	b Larwood	4	run out		0
	b 5 lb 1 w 2 nb 2	10	b 3 lb 1 w 4 nb 1		9
Total		228			191

	O	M	R	W	O	M	R	W
Larwood	20.3	2	52	2	15	2	50	2
Voce	20	3	54	3	15	2	47	2
Allen	17	3	41	2	12	1	44	2
Hammond	10	3	21	0	10.5	2	21	3
Bowes	19	2	50	1	4	0	20	0

ENGLAND

H. Sutcliffe	c Richardson b Wall	52	b O'Reilly		33
R.E.S. Wyatt	lbw b O'Reilly	13	lbw b O'Reilly		25
W.R. Hammond	b Wall	8	c O'Brien b O'Reilly		23
Nawab of Pataudi	b O'Reilly	15	c Fingleton b Ironmonger		5
M. Leyland	b O'Reilly	22	b Wall		19
D.R. Jardine	c Oldfield b Wall	1	c McCabe b Ironmonger		0
L.E.G. Ames	b Wall	4	c Fingleton b O'Reilly		2
G.O. Allen	c Richardson b O'Reilly	30	st Oldfield b Ironmonger		23
H. Larwood	b O'Reilly	9	c Wall b Ironmonger		4
W. Voce	c McCabe b Grimmett	6	c O'Brien b O'Reilly		0
W.E. Bowes	not out	4	not out		0
	b 1 lb 2 nb 2	5	lb 4 nb 1		5
Total		169			139

	O	M	R	W	O	M	R	W
Wall	21	4	52	4	8	2	23	1
O'Reilly	34.3	17	63	5	24	5	66	5
Grimmett	16	4	21	1	4	0	19	0
Ironmonger	14	4	28	0	19.1	8	26	4

Australia won by 111 runs.

7

THIRD TEST

In ten days' time they were at it again; and in the interval the already edgy atmosphere had become edgier. This relates not only to the natural dislike of the Australian public of seeing their national idols the prey of what they felt to be unwarrantable aggression, or to the even more natural dislike of the idols themselves of being at the receiving end; there was a general tension in the air, making itself felt as much in certain scratchy little episodes within the touring party itself as in more understandable public manifestations of displeasure. Larwood himself, keyed up no doubt beyond the normal, made what from his own frank account appears to be a mild exhibition of himself by refusing somewhat petulantly to be twelfth man in a country match a day or two after the end of the exhausting Second Test. After some awkward negotiation Jardine eventually made him take part as a player, not as twelfth man; Larwood confesses that he was 'a little distant' to Jardine for a day or two after. These small flaws in the surface smoothness add up perhaps to little enough — a mettlesome player at the heart of an unnaturally tense situation is tired and temporarily at odds with himself or the forces controlling him; that player's captain, too, equally mettlesome, equally tense, and not by nature the most tactfully imaginative of leaders of men; such a clash can be readily understood if not excused, but this is not the only rumoured difference reported between Jardine and some of his men; the cumulation of these inclines the observer to more than one question about the nature of his failures in personal relationship and how dangerous they could be. More publicly there were such incidents as an outspoken and clearly honest attack on leg-theory bowling delivered, in one instance at least, by an acting Mayor supposed to be welcoming the team at an official luncheon, at which he appears to have dispensed with the welcome and substituted the criticism instead — an action demanding for its efficacy both courage and tact, and (it would appear) embodying considerably more of the former than of the latter. Finally there was the episode of the Adelaide practice: for two days before the Test the two teams practised on the great ground itself and (rather oddly, it would seem) the public were allowed in to watch free of charge. One cannot help endorsing Jardine's own curt comment that the fact that no charge was made for admission might have been expected to place those who did attend under a more than ordinary obligation to behave themselves; which these rather ostentatiously did not, booing and yelling and demonstrating at the English players to such an extent that on the next day, the eve of the Test itself, the gates were not opened to casual spectators at all. With internal and external susceptibilities so quiveringly at stretch, it is not surprising that when the match itself began, as it did under a high hot sun and before a tremendous crowd, the situation was standing ready for some kind of eruption, small or great.

Australia made one change only, Ponsford returning to

displace O'Brien, a reasonable enough adjustment. England, on the other hand, a trifle shaken by their failure to counter the spin of O'Reilly and Ironmonger at a time when they had felt their batting to be a strong and reliable asset, decided to play a left-hander as part-neutraliser of the danger and introduced Eddie Paynter, who apart from a hundred in Tasmania had done nothing particular on the tour and had not looked like being given the chance to. To make way for him a leading batsman had to go, and after some hestitation Pataudi (who was, as it happened, on the down-and-down) was excluded and Wyatt, who had trembled in the balance along with him for a time, was retained. The other change was obvious: Verity for Bowes, thus restoring a semblance of balance to the attack.

Another change that might have been made was not; Jardine, owing to loss of confidence in his own batting form, insisted that the England Selection Committee seriously consider omitting him. The suggestion was noted and unanimously rejected. Jardine won the toss and after prolonged consideration and advice from his senior professionals went in first with Sutcliffe. It is not altogether clear what fundamental dissatisfactions urged him to this, neither Wyatt nor Leyland having, in all conscience, failed when they had opened — but it is true that he had himself done extremely well as an opener with Sutcliffe before, and later events were certainly to offer a partial justification for the move. On this occasion he had no reward: the lively wicket gave Wall and O'Reilly an unexpected lift and bite (Sutcliffe was hit on the shoulder, and the delighted acclamation would have brought the house down if it had been in a house) and a cross wind made direction difficult to gauge. Only 4 was on the board when Jardine was bowled off his pads; Hammond faced an over from Wall which included two sharp bouncers (which were reported as elicting a comment that if that was what the game was coming to he wanted no more of it); in the next over he attempted his celebrated thrash through the covers off the back foot, got a tickle only and was caught by Oldfield standing well back. Sutcliffe got one from O'Reilly that lifted sharply and was snapped up at short leg; and Ironmonger ran one straight through and clean bowled Ames. The score was 30, four of the most formidable batsmen were out, the game was but an hour old, and the crowd was beside itself with enthusiastic delight. Jardine attributes the collapse largely to unusual pitch resilience; Mailey, from the other side, to weak batting. The one was, no doubt, partly the result of the other: be that as it may, the débâcle brought several late-order batsmen hustling back into the dressing-room to change, and ushered the phlegmatic Leyland and Wyatt out into the middle to deal with whatever might be the unexpected dangers of a sudden precarious situation.

Jardine proclaimed, in his own account of the game, his relief that the last-minute decision in selection had favoured Wyatt; looking back over the perspective of the season I can only wonder that there was ever any hesitation at all. From the moment he joined Leyland, (and who better to greet an incoming partner in a crisis?) the earthquake stopped quaking, a temperate calm descended. The luncheon interval came, and after it the wicket seemed easier, more predictable, the batsmen found time for their strokes. Wall's early pace diminished; and while O'Reilly, Grimmett, and Ironmonger held firmly to their aggressive accuracy, the batsmen held no less firmly to their controlling techniques. And it was no mere defensive system, a stolid covering-up or playing cannily down the line; these batsmen, who possessed all the strokes, used them when appropriate. The score at lunch was 37; at tea it was 150, and no further wicket had fallen. Leyland had scored, as was usual with him, mainly by pulls and drives, and there was little reining back on account of the shaky start — when he felt that the ball under consideration needed to be hit for four, he hit it for four, regardless. Wyatt, too, showed certain quite uncharacteristic aggressions, driving straight and through the covers with fine freedom, and crowning his achievements with no fewer than three sixes off the meat, hooks mostly and executed coolly and with judgment. Nothing that Woodfull could do in the way of containment could in fact curb the scoring; a modified leg-trap, a variant on leg-theory — nothing penetrated or perturbed; and they had added 156, not only pricelessly but with character and elegance, before O'Reilly got through Leyland's back stroke with a quicker one. Ten runs later, at 196, Leyland was joined in the pavilion by his partner, who much to his own annoyance drove into Richardson's hands a half-volley that ought in his opinion to have gone for four. The substitution of Paynter for the cautious Pataudi seemed admirably justified when he started immediately to build on the Wyatt-Leyland foundation with aggression rather than defence, and with Allen a sound anchor-man he was mainly responsible for the hoisting of the score from mediocre to promising by the time the end of the day was in sight. The

pertinacious Grimmett got Allen lbw just before time, but
Paynter and Verity saw the day out at 236 for seven.
England, if not yet satisfied, were at least relieved.

The relief turned, on the second day, to renewed
confidence. The injection of Paynter's special brand of
whippy adventurousness into the even, not to say solemn,
tenor of English batsmanship was responsible for an exhilarating vitality in the tail, Paynter exploiting all the positive
strokes whether executed off the correct foot or not and
Verity's loyal solidity supplying a reliable foundation. They
were not separated until the score was 324, and the innings
closed for 341 soon after Paynter at 77 had failed to get
properly hold of a hard hook and been caught behind the
square-leg umpire. England got ready for fielding in a
reasonably contented state, justified to the extent that four
of her leading batsmen had scored 17 between them and that
the last six wickets had contrived to add 311; the most
effective bowler, oddly, was not one of the formidable
spinners, but the seam bowler Wall, whose record of five for
72 in 34 overs on an iron-hard wicket well deserved any
medals that were going.

All was now set, had everyone but known it, for some of
the ugliest moments in the history of Test cricket, Larwood
and Allen, bowling very fast and accurately, had the batsmen
in an immediately defensive mood, intensified when
Fingleton got a touch in Allen's first over and was caught at
the wicket for 0. Larwood, as well as Allen, had begun with
the orthodox off-side field, and with the score still standing
at only 1, with Bradman now at the non-striker's end, the last
ball of his second over stood sharply up off a length and hit

Woodfull a painful crack high up over the heart. It is clear
from the several accounts that the ball whipped back from
the off, that Woodfull, expecting it to pass normally and
harmlessly outside the off stump, had moved across his
wicket and lifted his bat out of harm's way and had been
surprised, if that is not too mild a word, by the abruptness of
the break-back. Woodfull not unnaturally staggered and
dropped his bat; all hell erupted with overwhelming violence
all round the ground; and Jardine, after a word of sympathy
with the batsman, walked down the pitch to Larwood. He
found him being encouraged by Hammond to take no notice
of the noise of trouble brewing, which suggests to the
dispassionate observer that the situation was promising to
disturb even Larwood's equanimity; and Jardine, not always
one would feel the most adroitly tactful of performers, added
his mite of reinforcement in the pointed words "Well bowled,
Harold," pitched in a tone designedly loud enough for the
non-striker, Bradman, to hear. Whether Woodfull heard them
too we are not told, but his subsequent reactions suggest that
he may have done. What is quite certain is that the communal
indignation seethed up to an angrier pitch than it had ever
reached before, and that what took place in the next few
minutes nearly blew the lid off for good.

As already carefully noted, it was Jardine's habitual
practice to start Larwood off with the normal off-side field
while the new ball was swinging to slip, and to switch over to
leg-theory as soon as the shine was off. The fact that as many
as two deliveries had bent in sharply as early as his second
over was the proximate reason for the next move. And now
there is a curious discrepancy in the published accounts of

the way that Larwood's third over began.

Jardine says, having remarked on the fact that the ball had turned back twice, "I was, accordingly, not surprised, when, at the start of his next over, Larwood made a sign to me that he wanted a leg-side field." All very reasonable. Now turn to Larwood's treatment of the same incident. "When I was on my way in to bowl the first ball of my third over to Woodfull, Jardine stopped me in mid-stride by clapping his hands, and motioned the field over to the leg side."

Well, whoever thought of it first, the deed was done; and nothing that had happened up to that moment matched the ferocity of the crowd's reaction. It is likely that any scientific explanation of the tactic would have been lost on most of them: all that they saw was that at the very moment after a batsman had been painfully disabled, the maximum heat was being coldly and deliberately turned up on him. This was one specific occasion when sound and fury really signified something; and that something has not been better or more graphically expressed than by Keith Miller and R.S. Whitington in their book entitled *Bumper*, written twenty years later but bringing this vivid scene before the eyes as scarifying as a horror film.

"Even old men of conservative habits," they say, "and normally most moderate tempers, seated in the Members' Enclosure, rose to their feet blood-red in the face as they first hooted and later, joined in chorus to count Larwood and Jardine "out". And for a time it was touch and go whether the less conservative barrackers on the opposite side of the ground would jump the fence and mob the English players. Men out on the Adelaide mounds that day say that if one

man had jumped the fence the whole huge crowd would have
followed him."

Let us perhaps be content that nobody took the plunge,
and that — miraculously as it may seem to the retrospective
observer ten thousand miles and now almost fifty years away
— calm was permitted to return to the scene. It is as well that
it did, because mounted police were ready if it had not. It is
sufficient at this stage to interpolate one comment only —
that if we lean over backwards to acquit Jardine and
Larwood of deliberate intimidation, it is asking the
impossible to clear them of the alternative charge of sheer
thick-witted stupidity. There are times in the progressive
survey of the events involved in this narrative when one
begins seriously to wonder whether the intellectual capacity
of Jardine, so patently paraded before his contemporaries
and his posterity, ever extended as far as plain common
sense. This is emphatically one of those moments, and his
subsequent remark that had he realized the misinterpretation
to which he was to be subjected he would never have set that
particular field for that particular over merely increases
rather than dispels our doubts about his judgment.

Woodfull happily recovered and continued his innings;
Bradman at the other end, now facing Larwood and Allen at
their fastest, was less assured than his rehabilitating hundred
seemed to have promised. Against the leg-theory he settled
deliberately for the bucking-and-weaving tactics which cost
him stability and poise and introduced a vulnerability into his
technique which (presumably) was the precise effect that
Jardine had all along proposed. He was timing Larwood far
less effectively than was the wounded Woodfull, who never

let mishap undermine him, and it was less of a surprise than usual when the great man turned a good length ball, not a bumper, neatly off his body and straight into the hands of a short leg with the score at only 18. McCabe went the same way only 16 runs later; and the score was barely in the fifties, when Woodfull, by this time near to exhaustion with the accumulations of shock, apprehension, responsibility and plain elemental courage, was clean bowled by Allen and departed for the dressing-room, where a little while later, during the brave stand between Ponsford and Richardson that saw the day out, he was discovered on the masseur's table by Plum Warner, manager and honoured envoy of the English touring party, on a solicitous visit to enquire after his well-being. And it was at this point that Woodfull delivered his spontaneous and monumental reply to his illustrious senior's query. "I don't want to see you, Mr. Warner. There are two teams out there; one is trying to play cricket and the other is not." In face of which protest, of which nobody can deny either the economy or the dignity, Warner had nothing to do but retire, in a distress that can be guessed at; the incident carrying the further sequel that this private communication became world-headline news next day, when somehow, and nobody has satisfactorily explained quite how, it was reported conspicuously in the Sunday papers.

It is no part of a chronicler's business to enter judgment upon Warner: merely to voice, as dispassionately as possible, a mild bewilderment. Here was one of the most knowledgeable and authoritative elder statesmen of the game who had committed himself in print only a few months before to an uncompromising condemnation of certain tactics and who was now manager of an International side whose captain was not only practising those tactics but actually refining and intensifying them. Warner said later in attempted extenuation that he had no control over his captain's tactics on the field. Even so, I find it difficult to believe that he did not try, and try without success, to persuade Jardine to modify his campaign. It is difficult to acquit him of an understandable but not ultimately defensible timidity. The tour must have been an intolerable experience for him, although I must confess that his own account of it seems cheerful enough; although later statements of his, made afterwards, will be examined in their place and may cast light on later developments. Meanwhile he continued to walk delicately, like Agag; and although, unlike Agag, he was not hewed in pieces before the Lord, there were some who felt that he ought to have been, and he himself there can be little doubt, felt as if it were actually happening. Jack Fingleton in a masterly chapter of his *Cricket Crisis* stated, and deplored, Warner's position once for all. There is nothing that can be added or subtracted.

Whatever backstage reverberations may have penetrated to the audience, the show was bound to go on: after a Sunday's excited perusal of the papers Ponsford and Richardson were there to face the barrage on Monday morning; and Larwood and Allen resumed where they had left off. Ponsford was a great batsman curiously uncertain in consistency in Tests, particularly on his home ground; he began this innings with a hurried snick off Allen into the waiting hands of Hammond, which the greatest slip-fielder of his time put straight on the grass. From that moment

Ponsford played with the circumspection and courage of his
true quality, and Richardson was the tough loyal partner that
so many more eminent batsmen than he were learning to
honour as more reliable than themselves. These two had
added over 50 on Saturday after Woodfull's departure: this
time they took their partnership to 80 before Allen bowled
Richardson, and Oldfield came in to play one of those
unexpectedly resourceful innings with which a wicket-keeper
so often confounds the hopes of opponents who have
temporarily overlooked the fact that he is also a capable
batsman. In fact he scored run for run with Ponsford for
much of the ensuring partnership, and they had confidently
and attractively added another 63, when Ponsford, once
more allowing his monumental confidence and technique to
be undermined by Voce's exploitation of leg theory, moved
too far over to the off and was bowled middle stump behind
his legs. Oldfield continued to attack and was beginning, with
the advent of the registered occupants of the rabbit-hutch, to
take perhaps unwarrantable risks; and one of these, sadly and
adventitiously, fired off another explosion. He tried a hook
off a shortish ball from Larwood − bowling to an off-side
field and pitching it on the off-stump − and the ball came off
the pitch a fraction slower than he expected, got a touch on
his bat as he swung round, and hit him on the right temple.

Oldfield did all he could; even as he collapsed in a heap
he found utterance to say it was his own fault. For this two
generations of cricketers hold him in honour. Larwood
himself acknowledges that he was sick with fright when the
batsman tumbled; the English fielders, with who knows what
fears and scruples and remorses bedevilling them, crowded in

to his aid. The Adelaide crowd, for the second time in the match, burst into animal roarings of abuse and vilification. Larwood himself confessed to a fear that they were going to "come at us." Maurice Tate, sitting in the members' enclosure, got up and went into the dressing-room with the remark "I'm getting out of here — somebody will get killed." It is a very great mercy that the damage was as relatively superficial as it was — and this is noted with apologies to Oldfield's concussion and hair-line fracture which kept him out of the rest of the Test and the next as well. There must be no minimisation of the shock and distress to Oldfield, but let us rejoice that his recovery was rapid and complete, and register relief that at a time when in the air Death moaned and sang nothing actually occurred to make its manifestation actual as well as metaphorical.

With the enforced departure of Oldfield the Australian innings broke up. The final total of 222 left England with a first innings lead of 119, as against a very formidable pile-up of ill-will, the latter by no means neutralised by the immediate appearance, along with Sutcliffe, of Jardine wearing his Harlequin cap, an emblem of deliberate exacerbation in an arena already tensed beyond the danger-point. The game re-started in an atmosphere of unlovely recrimination, but neither of these practised operators were of the kind to be disturbed by demonstrations, whatever their temper — although it is permissable to wonder whether the injudicious hook into which Sutcliffe was soon tempted, which got him beautifully caught by O'Brien the substitute fielder on the long-leg boundary with the score at no more than 7, may not have been the outward and visible sign of an inward and spiritual irritation on the part of a batsman normally impervious to emotion. After this momentary lapse, the English batting consolidated itself; Wyatt, drafted into the first-wicket down position (possibly with the idea of preserving Hammond until the shine had worn off), showed no sign of faltering, and he and Jardine played out the rest of the day with what even sympathetic observers thought was exaggerated patience. They actually took over two hours to add just over 70 before stumps were drawn, and Jardine made only 24 of these, playing bowling that looked less than hostile with a circumspection that called out a fine selection of the choicer abuse from the disaffected spectators. (On the occasion of drinks being brought out, one of these lifted up his voice and shouted "Don't give Jardine a drink! Let the bastard die of thirst!", which not only accorded well with contemporary public opinion but brought an approving wry smile from the England captain himself: credit marks to both sides.)

The next day saw a consistent continuation of these dour tactics, and the chief satisfaction to be drawn from it was the absence of any acrimonious incidents. Wyatt, who had played his part with great loyalty and effectiveness, missed his second fifty of the match by only one run, Jardine achieved his own half-century in four hours (out of nearly 150) and was l.b.w., and most of the day was taken up with a firmly-founded partnership between Hammond and Leyland, muted beyond their wont and kept on the steady defensive, confident but restrained, neither in danger but neither so much in command that he could unloose his aggressiveness. These two added 99, and the first time that Leyland tried to

MR. D. R. JARDINE

2. HAROLD LARWOOD IN ACTION

THE M.C.C. TEAM. BACK ROW (LEFT TO RIGHT): G.DUCKWORTH, T. MITCHELL, THE NAWAB OF PATAUDI, M. LEYLAND, H. LARWOOD, E. PAYNTER, W. FERGUSON (SCORER). MIDDLE ROW: P.F. WARNER (MANAGER), L.E.G. AMES, H. VERITY, W. VOCE, W.E. BOWES, F.R. BROWN, M.W. TATE, R.C.N. PALAIRET (MANAGER). SEATED: H. SUTCLIFFE, R.E.S. WYATT, D.R. JARDINE (CAPTAIN), G.O. ALLEN, W.R. HAMMOND.

4. FIRST TEST, SIDNEY: SUTCLIFFE PLAYS ON WITHOUT DISLODGING THE BAILS WATCHED BY V.Y.
RICHARDSON (SHORT LEG) AND C.V. GRIMMETT (POINT)

5. SECOND TEST, MELBOURNE: FINGLETON DUCKS UNDER A BALL FROM LARWOOD

6. SECOND TEST, MELBOURNE: BRADMAN BOWLED FIRST BALL BY BOWES

7. THIRD TEST, ADELAIDE: OLDFIELD, ATTEMPTING A HOOK, IS HIT ON THE HEAD BY LARWOOD. G.O. ALLEN AT FORWARD SHORT LEG

FOURTH TEST, BRISBANE: WOODFULL DUCKS UNDER A BALL FROM LARWOOD. THE CLASSIC CLOSE LEG FIELD CAN BE SEEN.

force it he was caught: then in the evening session Ames joined Hammond and played, as events turned out, his only really substantial innings of the series. These two, the lesser taking his time and tactic from the greater, were just beginning to release themselves from the day-long bondage and dictate the pace of the scoring, when with 51 up on their own partnership and the clock showing five minutes of the day to go, the bowling was entrusted to none other than Bradman. It is reported that Hammond, looking first at the bowler and then at the clock, went down the wicket to Ames, said in effect "Don't let up just because it's him, play as if he was a good bowler, we don't want to lose another wicket tonight," walked commandingly back to his own crease and was clean bowled next ball with a high full toss. "I have never" said Ames, "seen Wally so angry"; and we lesser mortals can at this distance of space and time permit ourselves a chuckle.

Hammond's 85, Jardine's 56, Wyatt's 49, Leyland's 42, all hoisted the cumulative total into the 300's, and next morning Ames with 69 and Verity with 40 helped to push it to 412 before the weary but persistent bowlers got their rest. They were a little fortunate in that Paynter had hurt his ankle, and batted at number ten, for that fierce aggressor was always a menace to tired bowlers: but all honour to the pertinacity of O'Reilly and Ironmonger in particular, who bowled more than 50 overs each and nailed back into watchful defence for the best part of two days some of the finest attacking batsmen in the world.

Even so, 532 was a fearsome target — almost, one would say, impossible; rendered, you would think, hopeless in the

first half hour when Larwood bowled the unfortunate
Fingleton for his second duck of the match and got Ponsford
caught at backward point before he had even thought of
setting his field for the leg theory attack. And indeed there is
no reason to postpone confirmation of the obvious: The
Australians had no chance and for the most part played as if
they were very well aware of it. Oldfield could not bat,
McCabe failed a second time, the tail folded without a
struggle, and (with two conspicuous reservations) the recognised batting dwindled to a single sterling effort by Victor
Richardson, as always refusing to lend himself to a panic.

The first of the two conspicuous reservations was
Bradman. Shielded once more from the number three
position, but not for long since Ponsford did not last, he
began with a brilliant abandon which he had not displayed
since the lighter moments of the English tour. He hooked and
cut with a crisp savagery anything that Larwood bowled
short — so long as the off-theory was maintained. It was in
fact in operation for longer than usual as Larwood had boot
trouble and was off the field for a while, leaving the coast
clear for Bradman to play dazzling tricks with the other
bowlers. Then when Larwood returned and switched to leg
theory, the brilliance gave way to the strange opportunist
swishing and weaving which has already been noted as the
deliberate Bradman counter to this special menace. He made
the best of his way to the other end as soon as might be and
continued a kind of high-temperatured euphoric assault on
the other bowlers. Needless to say the score bounded; he and
Woodfull had the 80 up in as many minutes, the hysteria of
both crowd and batsman mounted, culminating in a full-

blooded six off Verity (Bradman normally eschewed sixes, sensing unnecessary risk in the attempt) — soon after which Verity caught and bowled him from a hard drive. 100 for three, last man 66, and most of the crowd in raptures at the virtuosity. Not however, all; there were numerous dissentient voices, prominent among them the honoured and influential M.A. Noble, who broadcast on the same evening a stiff rebuke. "Bradman", he said, "suddenly developed a sensational desire to score off everything, and that regardless of the safety of his wicket. His opposition revelled in his indiscretions and laughed up their sleeves, because he was doing just what they wanted. Bradman evidently forgot that he was playing in a Test Match and that the winning of the game was paramount." It seems clear, however, that Bradman knew perfectly well what he was doing. He saw body-line as an attack which he had neither the time nor the inclination to master, and determined therefore to get all the runs he could, either off the leg-theory itself or off its alternatives, before it dismissed him. Furthermore he was not going to let it hit him; and for both the runs and the immunity he relied on opportunism and exceptional quickness of eye and foot. In a general vista of dour and defensive determination he cut a strange incongruous figure of cavorting brilliance, in the world but not of it.

The other conspicuous reservation was Woodfull. Slow and solid of temperament, concealing behind an aspect of mild benevolence a formidably tenacious obstinacy, he was unfitted either by skill or inclination for the glittering avoiding tactics that sustained his greater partner in his self-confidence. Woodfull had no alternative reply to the opposing attack than to stand up and face it, grimly. This he did, now, with virtually no hope of victory; bruised and battered from his first innings ordeal, with still more burdensome cares upon him after his encounter with Warner, Oldfield's mishap and further diplomatic developments stirring menacingly in the background, he went in first in the second innings and stayed there resolutely from beginning to end, four hours of it, narrowing his eyes and hunching his shoulders at everything the enemy threw at him. When the innings guttered to a stop at 193, with the fast bowlers virtually sharing the wickets, and nothing in the result to comfort Australia but its saving graces of resolution and independence, it was Woodfull who emerged undefeated at the end, 73 not out in four hours of grinding patience and weariness and unsubmissive courage. Whether Larwood and Voce bowled leg theory or off theory at him, he altered his cramped but well-tried defensive technique as little as he dared, taking what came with stubborn philosophical wariness, avoiding the bumpers when he could and letting them hit him when he couldn't. Australia lost by 338 runs, but Woodfull didn't lose. It is hard to think, even when reviewing the whole history of Test cricket, of a more sterling innings played by the captain of a side so disintegrated by a bewildered failure of morale. If anyone could have saved it, it had been Woodfull. If at that time it had been proposed and agreed to make Man of the Match awards to cheapen Test cricket, as it has later begun to do, I feel that it would have been Woodfull who should have been judged to deserve the medal this time — though perhaps it would have been a dubious honour even then, to have been named Man of what

has been authoritatively described in *Wisden* as the most
unpleasant Test Match ever played.

ENGLAND

H. Sutcliffe	c Wall b O'Reilly	9	c sub. b Wall	7
D.R. Jardine	b Wall	3	lbw b Ironmonger	56
W.R. Hammond	c Oldfield b Wall	2	b Bradman	85
L.E.G. Ames	b Ironmonger	3	b O'Reilly	69
M. Leyland	b O'Reilly	83	c Wall b Ironmonger . . .	42
R.E.S. Wyatt	c Richardson b Grimmett	78	c Wall b O'Reilly	49
E. Paynter	c Fingleton b Wall	77	not out	1
G.O. Allen	lbw b Grimmett	15	lbw b Grimmett	15
H. Verity	c Richardson b Wall . . .	45	lbw b O'Reilly	40
W. Voce	b Wall	8	b O'Reilly	8
H. Larwood	not out	3	c Bradman b Ironmonger	8
	b 1 lb 7 nb 7	15	b 17 lb 11 nb 4	32
Total		341		412

	O	M	R	W	O	M	R	W
Wall	34.1	10	72	5	29	6	75	1
O'Reilly	50	19	82	2	50.3	21	79	4
Ironmonger	20	6	50	1	57	21	87	3
Grimmett	28	6	94	2	35	9	74	1
McCabe	14	3	28	0	16	0	42	0
Bradman					4	0	23	1

AUSTRALIA

J.H. Fingleton	c Ames b Allen	0	b Larwood	0
W.M. Woodfull	b Allen	22	not out	73
D.G. Bradman	c Allen b Larwood	8	c & b Verity	66
S.J. McCabe	c Jardine b Larwood . . .	8	c Leyland b Allen	7
W.H. Ponsford	b Voce	85	c Jardine b Larwood . . .	3
V.Y. Richardson	b Allen	28	c Allen b Larwood	21
W.A. Oldfield	retired hurt	41	absent hurt	0
C.V. Grimmett	c Voce b Allen	10	b Allen	6
T.W. Wall	b Hammond	6	b Allen	0
W.J. O'Reilly	b Larwood	0	b Larwood	5
H. Ironmonger	not out	0	b Allen	0
	b 2 lb 11 nb 1	14	b 4 lb 2 w 1 nb 5	12
Total		222		193

	O	M	R	W	O	M	R	W
Larwood	25	6	55	3	19	3	71	4
Allen	23	4	71	4	17.2	5	50	4
Hammond	17.4	4	30	1	9	3	27	0
Voce	14	5	21	1	4	1	7	0
Verity	16	7	31	0	20	12	26	1

England won by 338 runs.

8

FURORE

So ended the Battle of Adelaide: a sorry enough business, it would seem, for most of those who played in it, watched it, read about it, heard about it. Viewed as dispassionately as possible, with the tumult and the shouting discounted as drastically as can be, it does not seem to have been a cricket match to remember and it was distinguished by few outstanding performances. The stand by Leyland and Wyatt which rescued England's first innings, the several contributions of Ponsford, Bradman and Woodfull, the unflagging pertinacity of O'Reilly, the sustained accuracy and penetration of Larwood and Allen — all these are on the credit side; but there was so much of characterless consolidation and sheer nerveless uncertainty about a great part of the cricket that the whole unbalanced contest cannot rate in the history of Test cricket above undistinguished mediocrity.

But behind the public spectacle and its attendant babel of intensified cat-calling, purposeful and unprecedented action was already being taken. On the last day but one, perhaps at the time when Woodfull and Bradman, in their so widely-differing ways, were each carrying the flag for Australia, the Australian Board of Control were preparing to crystallize national feeling into official utterance; and before the end of the day they had approved and despatched a celebrated telegram to the M.C.C., Lord's Cricket Ground, London, England. It seems that they did this in a hurry; but in not so breakneck a hurry that they had omitted beforehand to confront both of the M.C.C. tour managers, Warner and Palairet, with a direct request that they should put a stop to what was considered a dangerous and disastrous form of attack. On receiving the reply that the managers had no control over the captain in matters relating to the actual play, they sat down on the spot and concocted their formal protest. It was dated 18 January 1933, the last day but one of the Adelaide Test, and this is what it said:—

"Body-line bowling has assumed such proportions as to menace the best interests of the game, making protection of the body by the batsmen the main consideration. This is causing intensely bitter feeling between the players as well as injury. In our opinion it is unsportsmanlike. Unless stopped at once it is likely to upset the friendly relations existing between Australia and England."

A little jolted by this missive, the M.C.C. Committee went into immediate session. Not surprisingly, it took a day or two for them to reply; their response was not ready until 23 January, and when it came had a slightly intimidating opening and a rather frightening close:—

"We, Marylebone Cricket Club, deplore your cable. We deprecate your opinion that there has been unsportsmanlike play. We have fullest confidence in captain, team and managers and are convinced that they would do nothing to infringe either the Laws of Cricket or the spirit of the game. We have no evidence that our confidence has been misplaced. Much as we regret accidents to Woodfull and Oldfield, we understand that in neither case was the bowler to blame.

If the Australian Board of Control wish to propose a new Law or Rule, it shall receive our careful consideration in due course.

We hope the situation is not now as serious as your cable would seem to indicate, but if it is such as to jeopardise the good relations between English and Australian cricketers and you consider it desirable to cancel remainder of programme we would consent, but with great reluctance."

I think that it can be concluded that the last sentence of this missive shook the Australian Board of Control to its roots. It is hardly likely that at the time of the despatch of the first *billet-doux* they had had the summary cancellation of the tour in mind; at the best they could presumably have hoped for a peremptory instruction to Jardine from Headquarters to lay off leg theory at once, or else. This they did not get; one cannot help sympathizing with them, living as they were doing up to the neck and beyond in full and close awareness of the abnormal atmospheric pressures upon them and upon the players, and now receiving a brusque and not very conciliatory rejoinder from parties who had experienced nothing of the abnormalities which were now an unhappy commonplace to the original complaints. Nowadays there would first have been careful checkings on film; then, if necessary, brisk flights out from Heathrow. Not so in 1933; communication was over a vast distance; and the M.C.C. still sensed itself as *in loco parentis* to a froward child. Hence the *brusquerie,* and the consequent hurried retirement of the Australian Board of Control to prepared positions.

A week later, on 30 January 1933, they replied. (Perhaps it is salutary, a necessary re-establishment of proportion, to remind ourselves that this was the day on which Hitler came to power in Germany.)

"We, the Australian Board of Control", ran the cable, "appreciate your difficulty in dealing with the matter raised in our cable without having seen the actual play. We unanimously regard body-line bowling, as adopted in some of the games in the present series, as being opposed to the spirit of cricket, and unnecessarily dangerous to the players.

We are deeply concerned that the ideals of the game shall be protected and have therefore appointed a committee to report on the action necessary to eliminate such bowling from Australian cricket as from the beginning of the 1933-34 season.

We will forward a copy of the committee's recommendations for your consideration and, it is hoped, co-operation as to its application to all cricket. We do not consider it necessary to cancel remainder of programme."

An admirable rejoinder, one might think; harbouring in its first sentence a veiled and not unjustified recommendation that the M.C.C. refrain from authoritative pronouncements on matters of which it is of necessity ignorant: and in the last a dignified repudiation of any recourse to inflammatory action. The M.C.C. came back smartly for a further assurance: dating their next missive 2 February 1933:—

"We, the Committee of the Marylebone Cricket Club, note with pleasure that you do not consider it necessary to cancel the remainder of the programme, and that you are postponing the whole issue involved until after the present tour is completed. May we accept this as a clear indication that the good sportsmanship of our team is not in question?

We are sure you will appreciate how impossible it would be to play any Test Match in the spirit we all desire unless both sides were satisfied there was no reflection upon their sportsmanship.

When your recommendation reaches us it shall receive our most careful consideration and will be submitted to the Imperial Cricket Conference."

The storm is clearly subsiding, but the M.C.C. is equally clearly not yeilding an inch. The Board of Control, still it would seem a little scared at its own original foolhardiness, sealed and signed itself off on 8 February:—

"We do not regard the sportsmanship of your team as being in question.

Our position was fully considered at the recent meeting in Sydney and is as indicated in our cable of January 30.

It is the particular class of bowling referred to therein which we consider is not in the best interests of cricket, and in this view we understand we are supported by many eminent English cricketers.

We join heartily with you in hoping that the remaining

Tests will be played with the traditional good feeling."

It might perhaps be asked, as from a distance, precisely why, if the sportsmanship of the M.C.C. touring team was not in question, the Australians had thought fit to kick up such an almighty fuss about it. It might also be commented, as from the same distance, that it remained perfectly clear to all sane men that the Australians always believed, and continued to believe, that the body-line attack *was* unsporting. To this belief, whether it was justified or not, they had a perfect right, and were joined in it by numerous Englishmen. Their retraction before the M.C.C.'s insistence was no doubt a diplomatic one, and it is difficult to see that they could have held to their original accusation without acceding to the cancellation of the tour. This, incidentally, would seem to have been a logical enough step, if feeling was running as high as they said and if Jardine could not be persuaded to give up the practice. But that (speak not, whisper not) would have involved the authorities in incalculable financial loss. In addition, such a cancellation would have inflicted such a wound upon the time-honoured cricket relationship of England and Australia that it might not have healed yet. It is perhaps better that a little peremptoriness on one side and a little inconsistency on the other should remain on the face of a slightly confusing record to remind us of how easy it is for honourable men to make difficulties for themselves in hot blood and how far from easy it is for them to extricate themselves from it in cold, while continuing to remain honourable. These men, with the very best of intentions, did just that; and all was as well as could be expected.

Meanwhile, as the wires hummed and rumour occupied its many tongues with multifarious conjectures, for the most part baseless, the tour continued, giving happy opportunities for such as Duckworth, F.R. Brown, Mitchell, Maurice Tate *et al.* to display their talents and flex their muscles up country and elsewhere. Whispers of disaffection among the discarded units (known among themselves as "the Ground Staff" and concealing disappointment and/or resentment beneath a mask of carefree jocularity) had been among the least of the apocrypha in general circulation, and certain less innocent embroideries implicated one or other of the team members in open brawls with the captain. There is no need to suppose the truth of these any more than to discount them in their absolute entirety. Teams cannot go through exacting tours whose normal heavy routine is bedevilled, as this was, by unpredictable stresses such as harassed them all at this time without strain showing in some form or other. It is much to the credit of this set of tourists that ultimate loyalties prevailed as they did.

On Larwood in particular the pressures of publicity were particularly heavy; he seems at the time to have resisted them well and to have preserved balance to a very creditable degree. Ironically amused by the remark of a small child gaping at him as he visited a theatre one evening – "Mummy, he doesn't *look* like a murderer!", he kept his own counsel and walked alone. In a sense he did not feel responsible: he obeyed orders, served his captain faithfully, trained himself for the prime purpose of dismissing Australians in Tests, and left the rest to Jardine. One or two of the opposing sides

tried bowling fast leg-theory, or something like it, in a kind
of retaliatory reflex, and got little reward. The Victorian
tearaway fast bowler 'Bull' Alexander was included in a
Country XIII, oddly enough, to show what could be done in
reprisal form. He took one for 65 in eighteen overs. Eddie
Gilbert, the aboriginal from Queensland, who once got
Bradman out for 0, was propelled at the tourists in the hope
of them receiving something of their own treatment. Ames
and Allen comprehensively butchered him there and then,
and Larwood, bowling at a speed which made Gilbert look
medium-paced, took six Queensland wickets for 38 in eight
overs, and no leg-theory either. There was also the return
match against New South Wales, for which Larwood and
Voce were rested and Bradman, so to say, had a free hand.
Tommy Mitchell bowled him for 1 in the first innings, but in
the second Bradman saved his side from collapse on a less
than perfect wicket, making 71 with what *Wisden* calls 'a
curious mixture of good and bad strokes.' (It looks as if his
normal confidence was still eluding him.) New South Wales
pushed the tourists hard in this low-scoring match, but the
Englishmen won in the end, Hammond in one of his
occasional bursts of devastation taking nine wickets in the
match for 65.

On the whole the team approached the next Test in good
heart, one up in the Test series, confident for the most part
of their individual and corporate form and not unduly
unsettled by the storms raging about their heads. The last
telegram of the quoted series had been received at Lord's two
days before the next Test was due to begin, and in this
particular message was the withdrawal of the charge of bad

sportsmanship, without which it seems likely that Jardine would have refused to join battle. For the moment then, peace, or something like it, was restored, and the team went forward with confidence.

Larwood in particular cherished, as I think he had a right to cherish, a particular tribute from an unexpected quarter. It is only too true, whether it has been called to memory or not, that the name of Archie Jackson has not featured so far in the annals of this tour. It is one of the deepest regrets that any historian of cricket has to record, that after the season of 1930-31 first-class cricket never saw him again: progressive tuberculosis had hold of him and he disappeared from the scene a mere year or two before it killed him. He made a tough and brave end, as one would have expected — even playing a little cricket at a lower level, keeping closely in touch, lively and alert as he had been when in health. Only a few weeks before these stirring events he had been writing newspaper articles about leg-theory, which he was not disposed to malign. (The wicked might comment that he hadn't had to face it, but he could have replied that he had stood up to Larwood at his fastest at the Oval and what more did his critics ask?) At the height of Larwood's general unpopularity he had written, "Larwood is one of the most likeable and docile fellows one could wish to meet. He would not hurt a fly, and his success is the reward not of intimidation tactics, but of sheer skill combined with pluck and resource."

And to this most generous public tribute was added a few weeks later a further unsolicited private one. One the last day but one of the Adelaide Test — the very day, in fact, when the first of the controversial cables was being rushed together, when the tension both inside and outside the Adelaide Oval was being screwed tighter every hour and the excited crowd were giving the English all they knew whenever they saw the least excuse, Larwood was handed a telegram:—

"Congratulations magnificent bowling. Good luck all matches. Archie Jackson."

It was dated from a hospital in Brisbane; the time at which it came, to whom it came, from whom it came — all the cumulations of character and circumstance combine sadly, ironically, and yet reassuringly to make this incident the most moving focal moment of the whole prolonged ordeal.

9

FOURTH TEST

The teams arrived for the Brisbane Test in a cracking heat-wave; and as everyone who has experienced it will testify, a Brisbane heat-wave has a tropical ferocity about it that leaves the human metabolism limp and enervated. The tourists had just completed the State match against Queensland on the same ground, and Jardine harboured pertinent doubts about the ultimate durability of the wicket, clearly considering using an additional spin bowler in case it should tend to crumble on the fourth or fifth day. He was assisted in his choice by the unfitness of Voce — who had indeed made very little mark in the Adelaide game — and he replaced him with Tommy Mitchell, leaving the Adelaide victors otherwise intact. Australia, on the other hand, did a little desperate chopping; Grimmett, whose five wickets in the series had cost well over 300 runs, was discarded, and so was Fingleton, whose unfortunate pair at Adelaide seems to have obliterated from the selectors' minds his sterling 83 at Melbourne and his more than useful 26 and 40 at Sydney. Oldfield too had not yet fully recovered, so H.S.B. Love the New South Wales second string wicket-keeper got his chance; and the other places went to L.S. Darling and E.H. Bromley, two highly promising young Victorian batsmen (neither of whom was ever quite to fulfil that promise.) This gave the

Australian bowling department a slightly attenuated look, and discriminating prophets forecast untold burdens of work for Wall, O'Reilly and Ironmonger — rightly enough, since of the 265 overs that Australia were to bowl in this match, these three delivered 215.

However, they were not to be needed yet, for Jardine, to his great annoyance, lost the toss, and soon discovered that the pitch was without fire or life and that Larwood and Allen could get little help from it. Woodfull took Victor Richardson in with him, and not very many overs had been bowled before it became quite evident that not even Larwood's exceptional pace was going to extract any penetrating venom from such a dead wicket. Leg theory was tried, but was played with no great difficulty; both batsmen found it perfectly practicable to duck or to avoid. The heat, and the frustration, began to tell on Larwood; numerous rests and strategic switches of the attack by Jardine had no effect. The morning's inevitable barracking quietened down, died away; the crowd watched in contentment as the score was hoisted over the hundred mark. This was what they had come for.

The first wicket did not fall until half past three, with 133 on the board, Richardson's very free and fluent 83 being finished off smartly by a whippy piece of stumping. Bradman on arrival still seemed tentative against Larwood, even though the heat and the dead pitch were curbing the dreaded pace and lift; but after Woodfull's brave and solid innings ended with the side's score at 200, and McCabe after a few flashes of brilliance had been beautifully caught one-handed by Jardine in the gully, Bradman seemed to get into gear and

when time was called he and Ponsford were moving ominously along remembered tracks. 251 for 3 was no very
comforting overnight total for England to go to bed on.

Surprisingly, the scene perceptibly changed next
morning. It was just as hot, the wicket was just as lifeless, but
a night's rest had transformed Larwood from something
listless into something menacing, and Bradman's confidence
left him again. It is only during this tour that it can be said
that Bradman 71 not out overnight did not inevitably mean
Bradman 200 or so next day. He began the morning by
backing away as he had so often done before: and as so often
before he found himself defeated by sheer pace when instead
of standing his ground he stepped back clear of the wicket
and tried to cut a straight ball. This one hit his leg stump; and
only three runs later Ponsford did his own familiar avoidance
act, stepping outside the off-stump and being bowled
decisively round his legs. (Larwood, who had made a jocular
bet with some Pressmen after a late party the night before
that he would bowl Bradman inside three overs, no doubt
enjoyed the elation that all Fortune's favourites enjoy — for a
time.)

The downfall of the two illustrious masters let in the two
complete novices, Darling and Bromley; neither of them
ducked or shuffled, and when Larwood was rested each
played his colleagues with safety and resource; when
Larwood came back and was uncertain of his length they hit
him several times for four. They did not make many but they
made them sturdily and well; but when they were out the
innings stuttered and slumped, 251 for 3 became 340 all out
and Jardine was purring with satisfaction when they all came

off, having taken seven Australian wickets in half a day's play for only 89 runs. It was far too hot for anything in the way of lunch to be at all acceptable to the hardworking bowlers: and it is on record that their success was achieved on a carefully rationed administration of champagne.

On this heartening foundation Jardine and Sutcliffe proceeded to effect as monumental a structure for an innings as they could. Tenacious and impregnable, infinite in patience, devoid of nerves, they opposed with their impressive repertory of circumspect arts the entire range, from near-genius to mediocrity, of the Australian attack for the whole of the rest of that day. As anticipated, it was O'Reilly who bore the chief burden — nothing ever seemed to erode the stamina of this bowler, who for the next half-dozen years was to form the essential backbone of Australia's attack —, but Wall and Ironmonger provided accuracies and hostilities of their own — Wall particularly loosing a flight of bumpers at Sutcliffe (who apparently did not like them very much.) Jardine in this innings played as well as ever he did in the series, in which his batting for the most part disappointed him; and in this prolonged partnership he performed coolly and efficiently and so far as can be judged faultlessly, in contrast to Sutcliffe, who was edgy and uncertain, but whose vast experience and equable temperament preserved him from panic. For the last hour they concentrated entirely upon survival, and the game became virtually static: and when bad light stopped play ten minutes early with the score at 99 for no wicket, everybody, batsmen, fieldsmen, spectators alike, felt an alleviating relief. Jardine summed up the day's achievements by claiming that it was the greatest day that English cricket had known for twenty years. Ambitious claims, one would say, turning over in the memory certain phases of defiance and unexpected success in 1926 and 1928; but we need not grudge him his satisfaction, which was fully merited and carried an engaging personal pride as well. His general feeling of well-being however was sternly challenged during the evening, when Eddie Paynter reported intense throat discomfort and rising temperature, and little reassurance accrued from the doctor's diagnosis of acute tonsilitis, with immediate hospital treatment recommended. Luckily the next day was Sunday, which the patient spent in a kind of dopey daze punctuated by gargles, throat-painting and noisy visits from team-mates, but his temperature was still high enough on the Monday morning to occasion a definitive medical pronouncement that he was out of the Test Match altogether. Jardine, tempering sympathy and regret with annoyance that the victim, who had confessed too late to having felt off colour even before the match started, had not said so straight out in time to be replaced, began the day with Sutcliffe as dourly as he had left off on the Saturday night. He had planned, in concert with his main batsmen, to build the innings on a sure basis of disciplined defence and to leave it to two specific batsmen only, Hammond and Leyland, to concentrate if possible on attack, particularly against the formidable accuracy of Ironmonger and O'Reilly. Accordingly he and Sutcliffe dug in, taking no risks: and indeed, the first time that Jardine tried an adventurous stroke, with the total at 114, he mis-cued and gave a catch at the wicket. This let in Hammond; and the unfailing accuracy of the two spinners can be judged from the fact that this king of aggressive batsmen, with orders to attack, (and batting, according to the shrewd and perceptive Arthur Mailey, in his best form), was in for ninety minutes all told and could make only 20, including one hit for six.

Immediately after lunch Sutcliffe was out; Wyatt and Hammond, pinned to the crease, fought in vain to improve on a beginning which would lose its value unless built on, quickly. Only eight more runs came before Hammond misjudged a pull and was bowled; 165 for three was a far draughtier and less secure position than 114 for none had been, and when Wyatt was deceived by Ironmonger at 188 Australian tails were up and the disconcerted English were thrown hurriedly on to the defensive – the more so as Leyland, the second batsman to have hitting instructions, was finding it no easier than Hammond to obey them.

It was at about this stage that Eddie Paynter, swallowing gingerly in his hospital bed with the radio on, began to betray symptoms of ominous restlessness. Voce, who, it will be remembered, was out of the side owing to unfitness, had come companionably to listen to the commentary with him,* and as the scoring slowed and wickets began to fall, the visitor began to find it embarrassingly difficult to keep the patient in bed. Delirium was discounted, for it was likely that the visitor shared and sympathised with the patient's agitation, but no doubt formidable fears and scruples had to be surmounted before Paynter's peremptory insistence that

---

* This is taken from Paynter's own account. I have an alternative version from no less an authority than Bob Wyatt, who recalls positively that Voce had been sent by Jardine with instructions to fetch him.

Voce nip outside and whistle up a taxi persuaded the conspiracy into action. The invalid, equipping himself with dressing-gown and slippers, slunk furtively into the corridor on his way to the outer air and was fearsomely confronted by the Ward Sister. On his insistence that he was going to the cricket ground and that nothing she could do would stop him, she sternly forbade him to do any such thing and went off to summon an authoritative doctor. Upon which he very reasonably made himself scarce while her back was turned, and was in the taxi before further frustrations could delay him.

He was hardly a moment too soon; Leyland, doing his best to obey orders, had been caught in the deep at 198 — the fifth wicket gone, now, and 142 behind — and one may picture with amused pleasure the sensation caused by the arrival in the distracted dressing-room of a tottering figure in dressing-gown and slippers whom everyone, as far as the present day's cricket was concerned, had been instructed to give up for dead. In a whirl of excitement he was instantly commanded to get himself ready, pads and all, and he had hardly done up the last buckle when a roar from the crowd announced that yet another wicket (Allen's this time) had fallen, and no doubt still diffusing an agreeable odour of ether and iodoform, he was bundled down the pavilion steps into the baking sunlight.

Leslie Ames, the not-out batsman, nearly swooned when he saw Paynter coming in; and the crowd, when they recognised the little figure under the white sun-hat, gave him a notably generous welcome. He was still white and weak, but the tension of the moment concentrated his energies on the immediate task and the encouragement of the crowd and his fellow-players buoyed up his wilting strength. Larwood, coming in to join him when Ames got out (as he did quite soon — this was no day for England batsmen) has reported that the patient had the shakes and was even quieter than usual. He also recalled how considerate Woodfull was to him throughout his innings. It is essential, in a survey of this tempestuous series, to take special note of the gleams of sunlight that every now and then irradiate it.

Paynter, doggedly, and Larwood, aggressively, hoisted the total out of the depressing doldrums. Once again we must remind ourselves that it is a mistake to regard Larwood as a bowler only; he was a free and attractive middle-order batsman, and indeed was good enough to be included in his county side as a batsman alone at times in later seasons when injury inhibited his bowling. This time he turned on the combativeness, got 17 in his first ten minutes at the wicket, hit a six into the Members' Enclosure and did much to eradicate the memory of the inhibited stodginess that had shackled the progress of the earlier part of the England innings, bottled up Hammond and Leyland, and reduced Ames to 17 in an hour and a half.

Inspired by Larwood's example, and perhaps easing into a more normal equanimity with the gentle sweat and the exercise, Paynter began to bat with a little confidence and to make a few strokes of his own. It was a pity that Larwood hit over a yorker and was bowled just before the close, but Verity came in to play out time, which found Paynter happily weak at the knees with 24 not out, having been in while 55 very valuable runs were added. He staggered up the pavilion steps to a tumultuous welcome, fell into the nearest taxi and was conducted back to hospital, not all that happy about the prospect of an early reunion with the Ward Sister, but otherwise reasonably satisfied with his part in the rehabilitation. Most fortunately the Ward Sister turned out to be a kindred spirit disposed to applaud rather than to exact vengeance with a hypodermic needle, and any prospect of Aeschylean doom that might have disturbed him during his innings proved to be illusory; he was propelled into bed and sleep by a benevolent rather than an exacerbated hand.

Next morning, weighed down with bottles of gargle and prescribed tablets, he proceeded with firmer step and a much clearer head to resume the struggle. The balance of the match was still a very open question − 271 for 8 as against 340 was no state to breed hopeful optimism, and one false step would bring in Tommy Mitchell, who as a batsman rated as something rather later than the beginning of the end. Paynter was fortunate in his partner: there was no more reliable tail-ender than Verity, a watchful and temperate batsman with few of the graces but a great measure of solidity and shrewdness, and he it was who anchored the innings firmly at one end and left it to Paynter to ease himself into scoring form at the other. Not surprisingly, his bat had rather more edge than usual, but luck was with him and uppish shots fell clear of fieldsmen. More slowly than it would have done had Paynter been fully fit, the score heaved itself up through the 280's, the 290's, the 300's; Australia's frustrated attack, while containing ambitious aggression, was nevertheless losing, rather than confirming, its grip on the game. By lunch-time England, without losing any more wickets, were only 19 behind, and after lunch, without any increase in the tempo but with plenty of increase in confidence, the Australian total was overhauled; soon after which Paynter, with the gunpowder running out at the heels of his boots, gave an exhausted catch and retired amid tempestuous applause. The value of his innings was of course enormous: with the added melodramatic colouring it was hoisted at once into the regions of the legendary. Technically, no doubt, it had its limitations; but strategically it must take its place among the classic individual performances of the series. We must rescue a portion of the special praise for the tenacious Verity; their partnership of 92 was without any doubt the turning-point of the match, in which a victory for Australia would have squared the series and put no-one knows what intolerable strain upon the last Test which was only just over a week away. Yet while we celebrate these two batsmen let us remember to hold in equal honour O'Reilly, with his 67 overs for 120 runs and four wickets, and Ironmonger with his 43 overs for 69 runs and three wickets — prodigies of accuracy and patience, superb skills meanly rewarded.

Tommy Mitchell came in and out and England's lead was 16. By so little, and yet by so much, are crucial psychological advantages gained. Australia batted again under the cloud of an incipient inferiority complex, however firmly the aggressions of Victor Richardson at the outset appeared to deny this. He virtually usurped the scoring, took advantage of the unresponsive wicket and manfully and of intent made an attack on Larwood. Jardine sought to unsettle the openers by alternating his three pace bowlers, Larwood, Allen and Hammond, and giving each of them bewilderingly short spells, sometimes of one over only. The heat was of the heavily oppressive order, and it may be that in this way they tired less easily: the scheme was not greatly successful and Richardson in particular profited readily from anything short of a length: but he was caught going for a drive when he had made 32 out of 46, Woodfull playing a very minor role indeed.

Bradman was, for him in his current feverishness, unusually cautious: which, rightly enough, was interpreted by Jardine as an ominous sign. The dead wicket had certainly removed the vicious sting from the Larwood menace; Woodfull was playing him with steady certainty, and after amassing a number of singles here and there, Bradman eased himself into his true scoring vein by taking 12 off one of Larwood's overs, including two cracking square cuts of the most polished and satisfying order. Jardine, cannily noticing that although they had been precisely timed and placed they had both been given air, placed a deepish backward point for Larwood's next over and was rewarded by Bradman repeating the shot and holing out, a curious aberration, one would think, on the part of so accomplished a batsman.

This was at 79, with Australia now only 63 ahead; and two runs later Ponsford, glancing Allen off his legs from the meat of the bat, was marvellously caught by Larwood at leg slip, who hurled himself headlong and snatched it left-handed. And when, only ten runs on, Woodfull's tentative half-cock shot at Mitchell's leg spin carried to Hammond at slip, Australia at 91 for four had lost nearly all her grounds for confidence. McCabe and Darling saw the score to 108 before close of play, but there is no doubt that from the time of the double downfall of Bradman and Ponsford that night, England could regard themselves as having the match, and consequently the Ashes, in the bag.

The heavily oppressive weather of the first four days of this game was showing signs, by the time the fifth day's play began, of concentrating itself into thunder or rain, although this was a threat only and, for the time being, not an actuality. Foremost in the English intention, however, for this reason as much as for any other, was the determination to get the rest of the wickets quickly. For a time McCabe and Darling, formidable batsmen both, proceeded warily and without panic. Ever since the first Test, if not before it, the English had felt a healthy and proper respect for McCabe, and were naturally very keenly aware that a repetition of that classic performance would knock any rational set of plans endways. Relief, then, was publicly and joyfully expressed when the aggressive spirit (as often it did) triumphed over the young batsmen's discretion, and he was clean bowled trying to hook Verity, a dangerous adventure at the best of times. The two had seen the score to 136; and Darling and Bromley pushed it bravely to 163, after which resistance broke and all cohesion collapsed, a sad procession of batting failures decorating the early afternoon — the worst disaster, a deplorable middle-of-the-pitch mix-up between Darling and Love (ironic juxtaposition of names) which resulted in the running-out of Darling when well set, was symptomatic of the psychological breakdown affecting the whole team. The innings ended at 175, and England were consequently left with what looks like chicken-feed, a mere 160, to get to win the match.

It was, as might have been expected, a considerably tougher job than it looked, or than it looks now from a glance at the score-sheet. England eventually won by six wickets, and 162 for 4 looks healthy and easy and comfortable. This cursory inspection conceals the fact that when Sutcliffe got out very early the England batsmen found it very difficult to force the pace. O'Reilly and Ironmonger went on in the second innings from where they had left off in the first, Jardine himself took a matter of two hours and ten minutes to score 24 and neither Hammond nor Leyland, (deputed, it will be remembered, to cut loose and do the quick scoring while their colleagues consolidated), could break out of the fetters which had been laid on them from the very beginning. Hammond was in nearly an hour for 14; and Leyland, though ultimately it was his decisive and accomplished innings that made the result quite certain for his country, was tied down contrary to all his natural inclinations and was all but four hours in making the 86 that honours his name in the score book. The two formidable spinners contracted freedom and aggression to the utmost, contriving in the upshot that the 162 runs took England 80 overs to make; and it looks to the dispassionate observer as if it was only McCabe's humanity and kindness in serving up a few juicy full tosses on the last morning just as thin rain began to thicken over the Brisbane roofs that got the match over before a downpour that went on for two days dropped its heavy veils over the tropical scene. Paynter, the very proper recipient of the last of these full-tosses, hit it into the rain-cloud for six to finish the game; and departed to an enjoyable popping of champagne-corks in the England dressing-room where the winning of the series and the recapture of the Ashes were duly appreciated by (I am glad to say, in the context of this tour) both sides and their well-wishers. It is possible that by this time just a little of the nastier tension had gone out of the air; and it certainly seems as if this, the fourth Test, was a far better and more enjoyable contest than its sinister and unattractive predecessor.

To add an appropriately sombre note to an occasion which somehow seemed doomed not to lack its blacker constituents, Archie Jackson died in a Brisbane hospital, only a mile or two from where the match was being played, on the last day of the game. It is strange that he, who played in no match of this season or this series, should seem, when the long view is taken of its history, to have played a curiously intimate part in it. What is certain is that whatever the dissensions they were buried in the general regret for the loss of this potentially great player so tragically unfulfilled, this personality of unassuming grace and charm lost almost as soon as found.

There was a week left before the start of the fifth and last Test, to be played, as the first of them all had been, at Sydney. In the interval the tourists engaged in one three-day match, against a Northern Districts XI at Newcastle. This match was of no particular interest or importance in itself, and it seems to have been played with something less than Test-class concentration and expertise by the visitors, who dropped a lot of catches and ended a drawn game very much on the wrong side of the balance. It is only worth noting because a heretofore obscure Australian batsman named

Chipperfield made 152 for the home side, and because the tourists harboured among their chosen eleven not only the entire Ground Staff previously referred to but also Plum Warner and Jack Hobbs. This latter made 44, batting, says *Wisden*, with all his old skill. It must have imparted a sense of style and distinction to what sounds a somewhat perfunctory occasion. (It may be of pertinent interest to record that it was on this tour that a number of highly illustrious players turned out in some Press Charity match or other, and that Jack Hobbs and Charlie Macartney opened the innings for one of the sides, and that on Macartney's dismissal Hobbs was joined at the wicket by Bradman, an occasion on which everyone present should be entitled to some sort of Certificate of Honour that they could show to their grandchildren.)

This agreeable diversion gave most of the sterner combatants a rest. There can be no doubt that some of them needed it; laymen cannot always appreciate the intensity of the normal strains of Test cricket, multiplied considerably in the present series by the special circumstances of which we are all so very much aware. The attitudes of the Press and public had been, during the last difficult weeks, strangely ambivalent, as we have seen well illustrated in the case of the barrackers who screamed blue murder at Larwood during the day and wrote appreciative letters to him in the evenings. Many of the team appear to have enjoyed Australian friendship and hospitality as if nothing whatever had occurred to jolt the normal relationships of good will: but isolated incidents kept intruding into the evenness of the normal routines. On one occasion several of the party, strolling in broad daylight along a side road in Adelaide, were charged from the rear by a party of young Australian hooligans, Eddie Paynter being knocked headlong, luckily with no damage; at another moment after the fourth Test a number of them got involved in an argument in a hotel bar which culminated somewhat alarmingly in one of the Australian participants producing a revolver. Prompt action on the part of the landlord, coupled with indisputable evidence that the party of the first part was too drunk to hold the revolver, much less point it at Larwood (which was his incoherently-expressed intention), staved off disaster but did not lessen the sense of strain under which most of the tourists cannot have helped labouring during this last phase of their progress.

AUSTRALIA

V.Y. Richardson	st Ames b Hammond . . .	83	c Jardine b Verity 32
W.M. Woodfull	b Mitchell	67	c Hammond b Mitchell . 19
D.G. Bradman	b Larwood	76	c Mitchell b Larwood . . 24
S.J. McCabe	c Jardine b Allen	20	b Verity 22
W.H. Ponsford	b Larwood	19	c Larwood b Allen . . . 0
L.S. Darling	c Ames b Allen	17	run out 39
E.H. Bromley	c Verity b Larwood	26	c Hammond b Allen . . . 7
H.S. Love	lbw b Mitchell	5	lbw b Larwood 3
T.W. Wall	not out	6	c Jardine b Allen 2
W.J. O'Reilly	c Hammond b Larwood . .	6	b Larwood 4
H. Ironmonger	st Ames b Hammond . . .	8	not out 0
	b 5 lb 1 nb 1	7	b 13 lb 9 nb 1 23
Total		340	175

	O	M	R	W		O	M	R	W
Larwood	31	7	101	4		17.3	3	49	3
Allen	24	4	83	2		17	3	44	3
Hammond	23	5	61	2		10	4	18	0
Mitchell	16	5	49	2		5	0	11	1
Verity	27	12	39	0		19	6	30	2

ENGLAND

D.R. Jardine	c Love b O'Reilly	46	lbw b Ironmonger 24
H. Sutcliffe	lbw b O'Reilly	86	c Darling b Wall 2
W.R. Hammond	b McCabe	20	c Bromley b Ironmonger 14
R.E.S. Wyatt	c Love b Ironmonger . . .	12	
M. Leyland	c Bradman b O'Reilly . . .	12	c McCabe b O'Reilly . . 86
L.E.G. Ames	c Darling b Ironmonger . .	17	not out 14
G.O. Allen	c Love b Wall	13	
E. Paynter	c Richardson b Ironmonger	83	not out 14
H. Larwood	b McCabe	23	
H. Verity	not out	23	
T.B. Mitchell	lbw b O'Reilly	0	
	b 1 lb 12 nb 3	21	b 2 lb 4 nb 2 8
Total		356	(4 wkts) 162

	O	M	R	W		O	M	R	W
Wall	33	6	66	1		7	1	17	1
O'Reilly	67.4	27	120	4		30	11	65	1
Ironmonger	43	19	69	3		35	13	47	2
McCabe	23	7	40	2		7.4	2	25	0
Bromley	10	4	19	0					
Bradman	7	1	17	0					
Darling	2	0	4	0					

England won by 6 wickets.

10

FIFTH TEST

The first *piquant* preliminary note struck as this last major ordeal was preparing was an urgent and apparently more than half-serious request to Jardine by Larwood to rest him for the match. Not very surprisingly, Jardine turned it down; it is possible that had he agreed Larwood himself would have regretted having suggested it. It is mildly interesting to note it as further indication of the steam-heated pressures to which everyone was exposed at that time. Admittedly the prime object — the series, which in its turn incorporated the Ashes, if that were of real importance — had been achieved; but Jardine was the last man to relax in his efforts to beat, rather than contain, the Australians, and it is not easy, however liberally and objectively one might wish to view the situation, to disagree with him. A Test Match is there to be fought and won, not played with in an amused and off-hand manner.

Accordingly only one change was made in the England side. Voce, now completely recovered, was readmitted to his prescriptive place, and Mitchell was returned to store with due acknowledgments. He had done all that could have been expected of him, and retired full of honour. As for the Australians, an effort at rehabilitation was necessary, and their task was made more difficult by an injury to Tim Wall, whose fast bowling, while not quite in the Larwood class, had been of sterling value and dependability — and in fact, in the upshot, brought him more wickets and a slightly lower average than Ironmonger's, which is a good reason why he should be noted and not forgotten in the chronicle of this series. In his place was introduced a new fast bowler: not Lisle Nagel, who had been so successful earlier on but was now injured, but the tearaway 'Bull' Alexander from Victoria who, it will be remembered, had been ushered in to practise a form of leg-theory in a minor match and had been comprehensively thrashed. Oldfield, now recovered, was back behind the wicket; Bromley was (perhaps a little too sharply) dropped and the South Australian P.K. Lee, an off-spinner and capable middle-order batsman, introduced in his stead. Finally, and a little sadly, Ponsford lost his place for the second time in the series, and back came Leo O'Brien for a second try. The Australian selectors were, as it would seem by this time, understandably jumpy, and it is perhaps not easy in the light of history to justify all these spasmodic changes; but this is a common manoeuvre when a side has been caught on the wrong foot and is finding it difficult to resume its proper station on the right one.

The attendance at Sydney on the opening day was as good as could have been hoped for even if the Ashes had been still for the snatching; it was a lovely day and a hotly-fought Test match is a hotly-fought Test match, Ashes or no Ashes. Australia won the toss again, and lost the advantage almost at once when Richardson edged Larwood into the gully before a run had been scored. On Bradman's arrival Larwood perceptibly quickened his pace, but con-

tinued for longer than usual to bowl to an off-side field; he
found Bradman in an apparently perky and confident mood,
ready with the opportunist stroke when opportunism was
called for, and ominously sound when it was not. Woodfull at
the other end hunched himself into a virtually permanent
defensive posture, and after an over or two of unsuccessful
leg-theory Larwood was replaced by Allen and any serious
demonstration thereby avoided — for the time.

He was rested for half an hour, during which time
Bradman added 40 to his score; then he came back twenty
minutes before lunch to bowl to the now deeply-rooted pair,
Bradman the questing run-chaser, Woodfull the tenaciously-
entrenched defender dying by inches at his post; there was so
much varied skill contained in the persons of these two
masters — one a master in every way, the other a master of
his own restricted techniques but no less a master for that —
that a near-permanent stability appeared to have been
achieved. Yet Larwood, returning after his rest, bowled them
both in two overs — Woodfull, by forcing him to play on,
Bradman through an over-adventurous shot off a straight ball
much in the manner of his late disorganisation. This totalled
up to 64 for three and McCabe and O'Brien apparently very
ready to attack. The fortunes of Australia's batsmen were
materially assisted at this stage of the game by a disconcerting plague of dropped catches which broke out among
the Englishmen; a manifestation much deplored by Jardine,
who on the strength of five misses before lunch gave his team
a severe ticking-off during the interval, a disciplinary
corrective whose acknowledged value was abruptly discounted when the captain himself spilled a fairly easy catch

on to the grass in the first over afterwards. Neither Voce nor Allen of the acknowledged speed bowlers seemed able this time to generate the fiery aggressiveness that, body-line or no body-line, had been such a potent factor in the English supremacy in the series, and it was left to Larwood alone to sustain it at the expected level. In these circumstances McCabe and O'Brien settled in to play cheerful and combative cricket, the kind that everybody knew McCabe had it in him to play and were at the same time delighted to be able to welcome in O'Brien. Two more catches went down and one or two airy shots were lucky not to rate as chances, but the two adventurers piled on gracefully and optimistically until the partnership was worth 99. O'Brien's dismissal at 163 brought in yet another young optimist, Darling, who immediately signed his name in the book by being missed twice and continuing, in spite of that, to go boldly for all the runs he could get. He and McCabe, trading continually on the listlessness of the bowling and the unreliability of the catching, put up 81 for the next wicket before McCabe was unlucky enough to offer a catch that was held rather than dropped; and by the end of the day aggressiveness, courage and luck had hoisted the Australian score to 269 for five, a situation happier for them for the moment than any they had been able to relish since the second Test. What Jardine said to his ragged brigade in the dressing-room is not on record; what is clear from all accounts is that staleness had set in, upon nearly everyone except (mercifully) Larwood. Arthur Mailey, most sympathetic of Australian observers, said of this game that in effect he was the only bowler on the side – the world's greatest bowler, he called him, with emphasis.

The Australian batsmen continued next day to dictate terms, or at least to appear to do so. Surprisingly, Oldfield, happily recovered, was the one to provide the shrewd effective techniques and to be the central figure in the batting strategy. He played Larwood better than any of the others, and he inspired Darling, the more accomplished but less experienced batsman, with new confidence and resource. England dropped another catch or two, Larwood suffering the most and Oldfield being the chief beneficiary; Darling, going for his shots with increased authority, pushed his score along with an equal leaven of clean and streaky attacking strokes, until Verity finally bowled him with an unexpectedly fast yorker. Lee the newcomer, to everyone's mild surprise but emphatic pleasure, carried on where Darling left off and attacked the bowling with relish and success, seeming to care little for the fact that he was a kind of débutant, and duly qualifying for full adult membership of the club by being missed on the boundary before being caught off a skier after having made 42 out of 57. Australia could feel very happy at lunch with over 400 on the board with seven wickets down, and though Paynter immediately afterwards threw Oldfield out in the only creditable episode in the contemporary history of England's fielding, there were enjoyable and random passages of hitting and missing by O'Reilly and Alexander (and as far as missing was concerned, by at least two more English fielders) before the innings closed for 435. Chief honours in the out-cricket were taken by Larwood with a very creditable four for 98 in 32 overs, one of his finest and best-sustained pieces of bowling in the series: and marked in sombre black on the record should be the number of possible catches grassed by English fielders, fourteen.

When England batted the malaise was still in the air, and before the score had reached 30 Jardine had been twice missed in the slips. Alexander, who had come in for Wall, worked up a fair speed quite early, and he moved the ball sufficiently several times to find the edge of Jardine's bat, not an easy objective, a credit to be noted in his favour along with the fact, noted by Arthur Mailey, that he had Sutcliffe very ill at ease. (He also had Sutcliffe looking suspiciously at the footmarks of his follow-through.) Jardine, whose tenacity, courage and single-mindedness had never been more positive than they had in this series, had ironically not found it easy to strike his accustomed rich scoring vein, and although he had played a number of toughly resolute innings he had only once reached fifty; and now again he fell early, being this time brilliantly caught by Oldfield on the leg-side with his score at 18 and the total at only 31. Another quick wicket, and the odds would have swung in Australia's favour; but Sutcliffe and Hammond, heads down, batting tactics based on solid defensive techniques built up over years of experience, weathered an awkward few overs from Alexander and O'Reilly, and constructed on tried and reliable foundations the makings of a long innings. Jardine reports that Sutcliffe was playing like the tired man he was; Mailey notes that he was lucky to sky several shots on the leg-side where no fielders were near; *Wisden* says that he batted at his best, but was overshadowed by his partner. Whatever discrepancies there may be upon the record, it is sufficient to remember that for nearly three hours that day, as similarly in the first

Test of the series, the Sydney spectators were able to study in depth and in detail the complementary geniuses of Sutcliffe and Hammond — whether they liked it or not. Almost certainly the vast majority would have wished them both out in two balls, and this is fully understandable; but it may be that certain more discriminating watchers may have sensed that this kind of greatness is available but rarely, and even then rarely in double measure: the one all watchful but elegant impregnability, the other at the peak of his unique dynamic grace and power. And these watchers, their aesthetic pleasure at odds more than often with their patriotic inclinations, may have gone away that night with a heightened sense of pleasure in the measured skill of great batsmen transcending even the daunting nationalist barriers that no good will can altogether make away with. Sutcliffe and Hammond, the one pulling and hooking, the other driving off front foot and back, the prime powers and strengths of contemporary English batting displayed at their finest, set the English innings smoothly running like a finely-tuned engine and took the score to 122 before a fine catch by Richardson got rid of Sutcliffe.

Not many minutes remained before drawing of stumps; and Jardine, reasonably, sent in a night-watchman. Not so obviously reasonably, he had, some long time before the wicket fell, detailed Larwood to get his pads on. He addressed him in his customary laconic way while he was still cooling down under the shower, neither expecting nor accepting a no for an answer. Larwood, less docile off the field than on, made his views known to some of his fellows, expressing himself with some violence. The aforesaid fellows had their work cut out for a time patting him and calming him down; out in the middle Sutcliffe and Hammond went about their business, happily sustaining the waiting period long enough for the incensed bowler to accept the inevitable, get his pads on and address himself to the possible duties before him. When a roar outside heralded the fall of a wicket a few minutes before time he was not even watching the cricket; when a further curt word from the captain confirmed his original order, Larwood rose sulkily, told Leslie Ames to get his bat ready because he meant to get himself out at once, and stumped out to the wicket with that vengeful intention still upon him. In pursuance of this reprehensible purpose he attempted a suicidal run to Bradman (of all people) at cover, and only the fact that Bradman's bullet throw missed the wicket by a whisker and went for four overthrows saved him from ignominy and, no doubt, the dressing-down of a lifetime, only to be surpassed in virulence, it may be presumed, if his manoeuvre had resulted in the running out of Hammond. He survived: and stumps were pulled up at 159 for 2, a situation from which English supporters could extract a little reassurance.

This temperamental disturbance once more directs contemplation back upon the captain, in whose nature without any doubt resides the key to most if not all of the crucial turbulences of this series. Here is a captain whose central policy has largely relied for its success upon the ready and effective loyalty and co-operation of one highly-gifted player. This player has in the course of a gruelling tour complied so unquestioningly with his leader's special requirements as to bring himself world-wide prominence and, in the place where he is operating, highly unpleasant public notoriety, as well as physical near-exhaustion. This same captain, who one would have thought would have, for the purpose and in the particular circumstances, made a more than usually careful effort to extend to this player special sympathy and consideration, had already (in the 'twelfth man" incident shortly after the Second Test) been the cause of ill-temper and minor recrimination, and now, immediately upon the conclusion of a prolonged Australian innings during which the player had toiled with conspicuous dedication and success, detailed him without warning for a duty outside his normal routine and of (possibly) rather vital responsibility, and no reason given. It must of course be granted, and there is no answer to this, that the captain's word is law and that orders is at all times orders; it must also be concluded by any rational observer that Jardine was proving again and again that he had not got the first idea of how to handle human beings, more especially mettlesome and gifted human beings. We have already noticed an earlier occasion when Bill Bowes was driven to a quite frigid confrontation with his captain which could have been avoided perfectly simply if Jardine's apparently dictatorial intransigence had been accompanied by a civil explanation of what the hell he meant; and when we come to look at the present Larwood incident we find that Jardine accounts for his action very reasonably indeed by explaining that his idea was to let him get his innings over earlier in the English order than usual so as to ensure that his undoubted top excellence as a bowler could be fresh and ready for the Australian second innings. This is a proposition that Larwood would no doubt have been very willing to consider, if Jardine had had the common sense to realise that gifted players prefer not to be ordered about like defaulting soldiers on parade but respond more readily and valuably to ordinary civility. It is still very puzzling to know why Jardine, who cannot have helped noticing the reactions of his various interlocutors to happy little incidents like these, did not consider for a few moments what their reasons for their dissatisfactions could be.*

On this particular occasion, it would seem, the sun went down upon Larwood's wrath and rose again upon it next morning. "Next day," he says, "I was still batting on spleen." He is perhaps not quite as penitent as he should be, for after all it is only fair to remind ourselves that the quarrel, if that is what it amounted to, took two to make it, and it cannot be denied that Larwood permitted himself the tetchiness of genius, if one may put it charitably. Jardine had a perfect right, and Larwood knew it, to ask him to bat where Jardine pleased. The fact that he had exercised that right with an authority that smacked of the parade-ground was apparently still rankling with Larwood when he set out from the pavilion with Hammond to continue his innings in the morning; and any incentive towards aggression that was induced by the overnight freshness was agreeably reinforced by the tendency

* There is one other fact that should be taken into account here: I have it on the unquestionable authority of Bob Wyatt that the idea of sending in Larwood at this stage came in the first instance not from Jardine (whose choice would have been Verity) but from him — on the grounds that the weather forecasts hinted rain on the morrow and that the important thing was to get as many runs on the board as possible. I have considered this carefully and still do not think that this affects my opinion that it was not the decision itself that was mistaken, but Jardine's failure in tactful communication.

of the spectacular 'Bull' Alexander to do his best to hit Larwood with undisciplined bumpers. Alexander, a little o'erparted as a Test fast bowler, commanded speed at all times but length and direction something less than consistently, and whereas he had the day before contrived to contain Sutcliffe for a time, on this occasion he offered fewer problems. He was materially assisted in his inaccuracy by the enthusiastic Sydney crowd, for whom the spectacle of a menacing fast bowler bumping them at Larwood constituted the rarest of treats, and they were, to put it mildly, eager in their approval, which they conveyed in such elegant terms as "Knock his bloody head off, Bull!" and such kindred phrases as they were able to articulate through the saliva running out of the corners of their mouths. Ironically enough, this added to the enjoyment of Larwood's innings; Jardine and the Hillites between them had succeeded in injecting into his temper a combination of carelessness and defiance which, for once, manifested itself as a brilliant aggressive opportunism, and he found himself playing what can reasonably be labelled as the innings of his life. This is not the first time that it has been found necessary to call to mind his considerable capacity as a batsman, a stylist reinforced at times with power and judgment and resource, an admirable off-side player with corresponding strokes all round the wicket; today he was all these things with a mischievous devil introduced to direct operations. "Orthodox purists of the old school of off-side play", said Jardine of this day's first spell of cricket, "might have fancied themselves back with the giants of old. I do not imagine that R.H. Spooner, R.E. Foster, Trumper or Duff can have hit the ball harder or more cleanly and accurately on the off side than Hammond and Larwood did that morning."

In case this encomium should induce the idea that the mantle of Victor Trumper *et al.* had descended indifferently upon the shoulders of both these batsmen, it is only fair to quote the statement of Arthur Mailey that Hammond and Larwood scored at a run a minute, that they were "fairly comfortable", and that apart from an occasional beautiful off- or cover-drive from Hammond there was nothing in the cricket to cause the spectators to go into hysterics. It is of course quite possible that the glory of Hammond's off-drives, which nobody is going to dispute, so dazzled Jardine's approving eyes that Larwood's equally exhilarating aggression became credited with certain classical masteries that maybe it did not quite possess. Nevertheless there is no doubt whatever of the brilliantly assertive vitality of this innings of his. In the immensely valuable stand of 92 with Hammond, he did not merely match this master of aggressive batsmanship run for run: he scored almost precisely twice as fast. Ignoring any tendency to be disconcerted when O'Reilly beat him, which he did half a dozen times, he relied principally on hooks and cuts and slashes off the faster bowling and lofted drives off the slower, particularly off Lee the off-spinner. Lee had a reward for his refusal to be put off by this when he trapped Hammond l.b.w. just after he had come to his hundred, and contrived thereafter to worry Leyland with his spin, which of course ran sharply away from the left-hander's bat. Larwood, by this time, in the full euphoria of his good fortune and success, seemed to be beyond caring which way the ball spun or whether it spun at all, and added pace and volume to the promising stand between himself and Leyland by advancing down the wicket and hitting Lee for 14 runs in one over, including three fours. This brought the side's total above the 300 mark, with three wickets only lost, a remarkably heartening situation for an England side who had fielded rather despondently out to the highest Australian total of the series.

Leyland came down the wicket to Larwood a few moments later to suggest that he might like to go steady, adding that he had noticed, and that possibly Larwood hadn't, that his score was now 98. Larwood (and I quote his own account of this) replied "That's 98 too many," because, says he, "I was still annoyed with Jardine for sending me in after I had bowled so hard." This may be so, and we are at liberty to decide for ourselves whether we feel the continuance of his resentment to be reasonable: but what, I feel, can be taken for granted is that his annoyance must soon have been diverted abruptly from Jardine to himself, as almost immediately afterwards he allowed the thought of the century to inhibit the free flow of an intended on-drive, failed to hit it hard enough and was ironically caught at mid-on by Ironmonger, of whom as a fielder it was elegantly said that in the normal way he could not stop a tram.

As he turned for the pavilion, (so incalculable are the conflicts of emotion engendered by this game), every man, woman and child on the Sydney Cricket Ground rose and cheered. They were not applauding his dismissal or jeering at his failure to make the century; they were straightforwardly, generously and whole-heartedly honouring his innings. They gave him the full ovation all the way back: out of the same throats which only minutes before had been impugning his legitimacy and vengefully advocating his public dis-memberment they roared and counter-roared their tumult-uous congratulations. In the context of this blood-bespattered tour this is a quite astonishing incident. Students of crowd-psychology should incorporate it in their research-programmes. Yelling, whistling, laughing, crying, cheering, the great crowd stood as one man in salutation and gave their resounding accolade of honour to the chief object of their hate and scorn.

After he had vanished, possibly to a kind of reconciliation with his captain, the centre of the English innings experienced a precarious wobble. Wyatt was at one end, playing steadily but, according to most accounts, scratchily: nevertheless he stayed. At the other a series of middle-order batsmen got themselves out one after the other. Leyland got into a muddle and was run out when apparently well set and going promisingly; Ames, before he could get going at all, was brilliantly thrown out by Bradman (a doubtful decision, it appears); and Paynter was bowled by the hard-working Lee with England still 61 behind and only three wickets to fall. The batsman who abode securely in the breach was the inestimable G.O. Allen, a very formidable player to come in at number nine and a defender on this occasion whom Jardine must have been mightily relieved to be able to use in that position. His bowling in the Australian innings, hampered by a muscle-strain, had been un-characteristically expensive: now he made up for this with his own brand of tough resolution. Before stumps were drawn he and Wyatt had added 44 to the slightly tenuous total; and

although just before time Ironmonger made his day and
everyone else's by accepting a second catch, this time from
Wyatt for an extremely useful if otherwise undistinguished
51, Allen was still unbeaten with 25 and only 17 runs
separated the two teams.

And next morning Allen steered England safely ahead. He
had a little support from Verity before Alexander, who had
up till now taken considerable punishment with nothing to
show for it, got the Yorkshireman caught at the wicket, but
it was a last-wicket stand with a very competent-looking
Voce that established and increased the lead. Allen's admirable 48 was sealed off in the end by a brilliant Bradman
catch, and the half-way house was thereby attained with
England's nose in front all right, but only by a trifling matter
of 19. O'Reilly and Lee came off the field with most bowling
credit, the newcomer with four for 111 doing marginally
better than O'Reilly's three for 100 — but as had been true of
England's bowlers, neither of them had much to thank their
fielders for at the end of this unusally enervating series.

Bradman's   brilliance   had   an   almost   immediate
opportunity to show itself again, sharp on the heels of his
catch; for the ill-fated Richardson, whose score in the first
innings must have been fresh in his mind if in nobody else's,
tried an injudicious hook off Larwood's second ball and was
neatly caught by Allen at short square leg. And it was now
that Woodfull and Bradman came together for what could
have been, and should have been, and for a very long and
testing time looked very much like being, the crucial
partnership of the match. Woodfull of course was his
predictably consistent self, unblinkingly facing the expresses

with a solidity that the upheavals of a few weeks before do not seem to have disturbed. Bradman began with the patent intention of meeting violence with violence, and runs came more freely than usual, more than a run a minute accruing from the twenty-five minutes play that remained to them before lunch. Larwood and Voce, both switching from off- to leg-theory and back again, found for the present no immediately apparent vulnerability. Woodfull shrugged off a bouncer that hit him on the shoulder; on the whole the bowling was directed well up to the batsmen.

After lunch the pace quickened, the score moved smoothly upwards. Most eye-witnesses visit Bradman with high credit for his effective parrying of the dreaded pace-bowlers: "He was standing up to it", says Mailey "magnificently .... and Woodfull, too, seemed to be playing with much more confidence." Fingleton, on the other hand, reports this innings with a characteristic cool detachment. "Cricket", he says, "has not known a more Alice-in-Wonderland innings than that played by Bradman ..... When Larwood was still two or three yards from delivering the ball, Bradman was on the move .... first to the off, then to the leg ..... barely a stroke he made was known to the text book .... it was the riskiest and most thrilling batting imaginable, and that in a limitless Test in which the sum total of risks, ordinarily, would be counted on the fingers of one hand."

The plain truth is that Bradman was adopting in cold blood a tactic which gave the impression and had the effect of a caper effected in hot blood. It is not really possible to decide scientifically whether a risky stroke made intentionally by Bradman in pursuance of a carefully thought-out policy was more or less dangerous than the same risky stroke made by any other batsman you would care to mention on the excited spur of the moment. I am prepared to believe that any shot made by Bradman had a better chance of succeeding in its object than any shot made by anyone else, and that it is in fact possible to concede that Bradman's performance was a good deal less risky than it looked. It is possible that the true danger to Australian confidence lay in the clear realisation that the body-line tactic had overset the superb impregnability which he had built up over the last few seasons and forced his resort to a brilliant improvisation which nearly all of his co-mates and brothers in adversity knew very well was beyond them. Even his partial success — and there can be no doubt that it *was* a partial success — amounted to a tacit confession of defeat — and defeat, even of this kind, was a partial failure. And this failure, even a partial failure, was the prime object of Jardine's whole exercise. Bradman's improvisations prolonged his innings and his contributions to the score-book; but it is by no means clear that they added very positively to his colleagues' confidence. It can be argued that by not succeeding in doing this, a batsman of his abilities failed in one of his prime functions.

Perhaps 'failure' here is too misleading a word; Bradman and Woodfull were in this second-wicket partnership tilting the game's balance very perceptibly in favour of Australia. Even as he watched Bradman's eccentric aggressions, Jardine must have told himself that, heartening as it may have been to feel that he had forced this batsman to an agonising reappraisal of his technique, it would have been still more heartening if the reappraisal had been more agonised and less productive. He tried nearly all his bowlers at Bradman, and of course at Woodfull, without avail; the shock tactics of one and the sober defensive imperviousness of the other were increasing Australia's lead every over. The hundred went up, and still there was only one wicket down; and the batsmen lined up to follow were all capable, and had every one of them shown himself capable in the first innings, of building solidly and substantially on a firm foundation like this. And it was at this point that, disconcertingly and unexpectedly, Larwood suddenly went lame.

There had been no warning of this. Larwood himself gives no hint that he ever felt any trouble before this innings began; indeed he underlines his keenness to get as much bowling as he could, for when he got Richardson he took his 33rd wicket of the series, and Maurice Tate's record of 38 was in his sights. He began by bowling very fast and very aggressively, (hitting Bradman once — the only time he registered a hit on him in the series) and now when his left foot began to feel sore he found it necessary to slow up. Then after a few more overs a sudden severe pain halted him in his run-up.

Here Jardine must needs make another scene. Although Larwood could barely walk he made him finish the over, which he did from a standing position to Woodfull (who without fuss played every ball straight back to the bowler), and even then would not let him leave the field immediately. "You can't go off", Larwood quotes Jardine as saying, nodding towards Woodfull's partner, "while this little bastard's in." I must confess to finding it difficult to know why, even though Larwood himself appears to agree and to admire what he calls the 'psychological astuteness' which would not allow Larwood to go off while Bradman was still there. Did Jardine intend to keep him limping around in agony even if Bradman made 250, which could hardly have been considered beyond his powers, particularly with Larwood withdrawn from the attack? Luckily for Larwood, and luckily for England, the element of rashness necessarily attendant upon Bradman's new techniques led him two or three overs later to play a wild shot against Verity, who bowled him with a ball of quicker pace, cleverly disguised. The score was 115, of which Bradman had made 71; and as on his dismissal Jardine graciously permitted Larwood to leave the field if he could still walk, Larwood and Bradman entered the pavilion together, neither of them (Larwood laconically reports) speaking a word to the other.

Getting rid of Bradman gave an immense fillip to English morale; although in the first innings as many as four of his successors had amassed higher scores than his, and there was no reason why this should not happen again, his departure always meant an access of hope. And on this particular occasion this was assisted by the ironic presence of the footmarks on the wicket made by the tearaway Alexander, about which muted complaints had already been made by some of the English batsmen. As it happened, these footmarks coincided with Verity's length, and Verity, with a clear run for almost the first time in the series, proceeded to destroy the Australian batting in a devastating spell of accurate spin bowling, which of late the Australians had presumably had little practice in playing.

Voce in fact began the collapse, after Larwood's departure, but it was Verity who disintegrated the morale of the Australian batsmen, or at least all of them except Woodfull, who gave yet another of those priceless defensive displays so characteristic of this admirable batsman, the personification of patience, reliability, and self-abnegation. Few players emerge from this series with more positive credit than Woodfull; so long as he was batting there could never be any certainty of England conclusively dominating Australia, and here again he was the only one to counter Verity effectively. After Bradman's dismissal eight wickets fell for 67 runs, with nobody but Woodfull and, for an over or two, the versatile Lee, who could offer any kind of opposition. Voce and Allen picked up a couple of wickets each; but Verity, with five for 33 in 19 overs, achieved his most impressive performance of the series; one which was without much doubt the decisive factor in this particular match. To get this formidable batting side out in less than a day was as unexpected as it was creditable.

This left England 164 to win, and it would seem that quiet optimism would normally have been the appropriate mood in which this reasonably modest task could be faced. Nevertheless, Jardine had it very much in mind that where Verity could pitch the ball, there could Ironmonger also; and the longer a match lasts the more susceptible a wicket is likely to be to potent spin, particularly when, as in the present case, the roughness artificially imparted to it by an irresponsible bowler in the first innings could very readily and immediately be suitably accentuated by the same bowler here and now in the second. For this reason and for others, Jardine decided not to risk Sutcliffe that night, so took the experienced Wyatt in with him to open the England second innings; and without any delay whatever encountered a little more temperamental difficulty. Right away Alexander started to cut up the wicket on his follow-through; right away Jardine called his, and Woodfull's, attention to it. (Nowadays umpires would be considerably firmer on this point than they were then: but that is another story.) The ensuing conversation resulted, it seems quite clear, in Alexander losing his temper, and when Jardine arrived at the other end to face him, bowling very fast and short at him. The crowd, which had vociferously booed Jardine when he made his protest, as vociferously encouraged the bowler in his spectacular reactions; and when a particularly vicious bumper hit Jardine a crippling blow on the hip-bone, their delight could be heard and shared many miles away. Jardine, being Jardine, refused to be unsettled; rigidly upright as always, he insisted on resuming his innings at once, which one imagines he would have done even if his leg had fallen off. Outwardly unperturbed, he played out the last few overs with Wyatt, stalked back stony-faced to the dressing-room, and only then revealed with reluctance as he collapsed on to the masseur's table that the ball had cut a gash across his hip bone and that he was sticky with blood. Of this incident he makes no mention whatever in his account of the game. Larwood, relating it, comments a trifle disingenuously that the sight of Jardine's injury suddenly brought home to him what he himself had done to some of the Australian batsmen.

Jardine, however, was not materially diverted from his

prime purpose by this, and was ready and waiting to resume with Wyatt first thing next morning. Steadily as they proceeded, notching up the necessary runs with circumspection, it soon became clear to him that, whatever the innocence of his intentions, Alexander had certainly contrived to rough up the wicket to the great advantage of the accurate Ironmonger, who was finding a length on the awkward spot and, what was more important, spinning it with an unpleasant and dangerous lift — a very potent and menacing spinner, this bowler, (even within spit and sight of his fiftieth birthday, which he duly reached about six weeks later.) Jardine accordingly decided to take every opportunity of hitting him into the empty outfield rather than be pinned to the back foot inside a treacherous crease, and in so doing got an early edge and gave a slip catch. His natural annoyance at his own failure to carry out his own intentions efficiently was then injected with a mild alarm when Leyland, sent in next because he was left-handed and would be on that account less vulnerable to Ironmonger's natural spin, played two extremely testing maiden overs from him and was then beaten all ends up by one that turned very sharply and bowled him off his pads. 43 for two might have meant one thing and might have meant the other, but it was in any case a great deal less healthy than 43 for no wicket, and for the moment Jardine may be excused for experiencing natural qualms.

He need not have worried; there was too little elbow-room for Australian manipulation, Ironmonger for all his skills was disinclined to pitch the ball far enough up to do real damage since 'buying wickets' was out of the question, and Jardine had at his command two or three of the most reliable batsmen in the world. As it happened Sutcliffe was not needed at all, nor Ames nor Paynter nor Allen — the list goes on and could have included Larwood, whose bruised foot might have prevented him from batting anyway. Hammond and Wyatt did all that was needed; when they came together there were still 121 to get, and as I have made clear there was no question of an easy passage, particularly when O'Reilly was in the attack, and was being so admirably assisted by the penetrating Ironmonger, (or should it on this occasion be the other way round?). These two bowled as tight as they knew; and what they knew as well was that they had up against them two of the toughest and least dislodgeable batsmen in contemporary creation, whose defences were solid and heartbreaking, and who knew only too well what to do with a loose ball. Hammond and Wyatt, high-class campaigners both, did nothing rash, they watched every variation of pace and flight with narrowed and appraising eyes, they took singles and twos here and there, they built confidence on circumspection and performance upon confidence, a stand began to form itself. Woodfull, watching their cool and unworried deployments of skill and technique and their gradual exchange of methods of attack for methods of defence, must quite early on have pushed any hope of a sudden reversal of fortune far back into a lost limbo. Ominously the runs started to flow, ominously Wyatt's defensive shots began to become scoring strokes, even more ominously Hammond unshipped every now and again one of his powered off-drives. All of a sudden Hammond took two steps down the wicket and hit O'Reilly for six with one of the biggest and furthest-carrying hits ever seen at Sydney; this released any inhibitions with which he may very properly have felt he had to check himself earlier, and from that moment there was no-one else in the game. The loyal and reliable Wyatt did all that was required of him, was in no way behind his partner in seizing opportunities for scoring, and when they came he seized them: but Hammond hit fours where Wyatt hit twos and all else to correspond, and no doubt Wyatt let him have all the bowling he could get — the match and the series came to a resounding and majestic end with a display of glorious fluent driving of the vintage quality that we associate with that great batsman, and the supreme culmination, the last shot of all that decided the match and proclaimed the series as England's by four victories to one, was a magnificent soaring six off Lee, a long climbing off-drive that hung in the heavens and disappeared into the unknown. Nothing became this series like the very end of it; a superb Hammond innings signed off with a characteristic Hammond flourish, as if all the disagreement and ill-will could be whistled away with a grand gesture and be forgotten.

Unhappily it was not as easy as that; but perhaps there was a little symbolism in the final burst of energy and grace. Once the strenuous fight was over there would be time to think again; to consider in coolness a situation that up to now could only be coped with in heat.

When Larwood left the field, in mute and distrustful association with Bradman, he did not know it, but he was leaving Test cricket for ever. The fierce pressure put on his foot by the constant pounding on the rock-hard wickets had not only bruised it extensively but cracked a small bone. This put him straight away out of the remainder of the tour, and had a crucial effect on the pattern of his bowling for the rest of his career. In addition, the fierce pressure put upon his highly-charged temperament by the recurring public and private crises resulting from Jardine's single-minded persuit of his pet policy was to be the root cause of certain subsequent eruptions, to be detailed in due order, which were to involve his complete withdrawal from the Test scene and affect the careers of other players as well. It could be said that for one reason and another the very exploitation of his own superb skill resulted in his destruction as a force in the field which he had come to dominate, and indirectly, as will be seen later, effected the entire re-organisation of his career and manner of life. Whether this ought to have happened is no profitable matter of discussion now; the fact is that it did, and has to be taken into account in reckoning up the advantages and disadvantages of Jardine's policy.

Thus the series came to its appointed end; an end which most of those taking part in it seemed frankly to welcome, so burdensome a strain had it become. There were two matches still left on the fixture list before the team departed for New Zealand, first-class State matches both (Victoria and South Australia) which in the objective light of reason one would have supposed the touring side to be too anti-climactically exhausted to face with much pleasure or confidence: but they gave the Ground Staff the belated opportunity to deploy their skills once, or rather twice, more. Tate made 94 not out, Bowes and Freddie Brown collected a few wickets. Of the Test regulars, everybody got some runs, Hammond gave Fleetwood-Smith another severe thrashing, but rough minor justice was done when Fleetwood-Smith got him out. Victor Richardson got his third duck in succession against the tourists; South Australia tried leg-theory against Leyland and Jardine and were made there and then to wish they had never been born. Darling got a very fine hundred for Victoria; Grimmett appearing for South Australia was once again so badly belaboured that it is a welcome surprise to see him bob up again in the 1934 series in England and exert all his old domination. The Victoria match, it is reported, was played in an admirably carefree spirit − it may be mentioned, as it were out of the side of the mouth, that neither Jardine nor Woodfull were playing − and ended, rather agreeably, in a tie; by contrast the South Australian game petered out on an apathetic last day, the English being apparently too tired to get the not very powerful side out. In these scraps and shavings the ordered structure of the tour disintegrated. A day or two later the party, minus Larwood and Pataudi, who had elected to go straight home, left for New Zealand; and it must regrettably be recorded that not a single member of the Australian Test side came to see them off.

The New Zealand tour consisted of three matches only: one against Wellington and the other two full-fledged Tests, at Christchurch and Auckland. They were all of them thronged with highly enthusiastic spectators in vast numbers: they were all of them ruined by rain. They were all of them one-sided and inconclusive; they were all of them dominated by Hammond. In the Wellington game he made top score (58) though he had to bat with a runner because of a septic knee; in the first Test he came in after Sutcliffe had been out for nothing in the first over, was missed in the slips at once, watched Paynter get out for nothing in the second over and then contributed 227 to his side's score of 560 for seven; Ames got a century and there were numerous other solid contributions. New Zealand's follow-on after a mediocre first innings was washed out before it had well started. In the second Test New Zealand, beginning precisely as England had begun in the first by losing two wickets for 0, never recovered and were out for 158; Hammond, coming in first wicket down at 56, proceeded to make 336 not out, then the highest score ever made in a Test match, in only five and a quarter hours, out of 548 for seven, a display of quite devastating mastery that even he never equalled quantitatively, and perhaps only once or twice in the matter of quality. Once again the rain descended with sombre finality upon a game that was destined to be an English walk-over; and the tour came to a damp conclusion. Such members of the party as had not already set off on separate homeward journeys proceeded thereafter on an agreeable voyage across the Pacific and so back via the American continent, fetching up finally in the homeland after a prolonged and chequered Odyssey which took them round the world in something rather more than a hundred and eighty days.

AUSTRALIA

V.Y. Richardson	c Jardine b Larwood . . .	0	c Allen b Larwood	0
W.M. Woodfull	b Larwood	14	b Allen	67
D.G. Bradman	b Larwood	48	b Verity	71
L.P. O'Brien	c Larwood b Voce	61	c Verity b Voce	5
S.J. McCabe	c Hammond b Verity . .	73	c Jardine b Voce	4
L.S. Darling	b Verity . . . . ,. .	85	c Wyatt b Verity	7
W.A. Oldfield	run out	52	c Wyatt b Verity	5
P.K. Lee	c Jardine b Verity	42	b Allen	15
W.J. O'Reilly	b Allen	19	b Verity	1
H.H. Alexander	not out	17	lbw b Verity	0
H. Ironmonger	b Larwood	1	not out	0
	b 13 lb 9 w 1	23	b 4 lb 3	7
Total		435		182

	O	M	R	W	O	M	R	W
Larwood	32.2	10	98	4	11	0	44	1
Voce	24	4	80	1	10	0	34	2
Allen	25	1	128	1	11.4	2	54	2
Verity	17	3	62	3	19	9	33	5
Wyatt	2	0	12	0				

ENGLAND

D.R. Jardine	c Oldfield b O'Reilly . .	18	c Richardson b Ironmonger	24
H. Sutcliffe	c Richardson b O'Reilly .	56		
W.R. Hammond	lbw b Lee	101	not out	75
H. Larwood	c Ironmonger b Lee . . .	98		
M. Leyland	run out	42	b Ironmonger	0
R.E.S. Wyatt	c Ironmonger b O'Reilly	51	not out	61
L.E.G. Ames	run out	4		
E. Paynter	b Lee	9		
G.O. Allen	c Bradman b Lee	48		
H. Verity	c Oldfield b Alexander .	4		
W. Voce	not out	7		
	b 7 lb 7 nb 2	16	b 6 lb 1 nb 1	8
Total		454	(2 wkts)	168

	O	M	R	W	O	M	R	W
Alexander	35	1	129	1	11	2	25	0
McCabe	12	1	27	0	5	2	10	0
O'Reilly	45	7	100	3	15	5	32	0
Ironmonger	31	13	64	0	26	12	34	2
Lee	40.2	11	111	4	12.2	3	52	0
Darling	7	5	3	0	2	0	7	0
Bradman	1	0	4	0				

England won by 8 wickets.

11

THE AFTERMATH

"But that apart", the reporter is said to have asked the President's wife after her husband had been shot dead by her side in the box at the theatre, "that apart, what was your opinion of the *play*, Mrs. Lincoln?" To anyone attempting a dispassionate summing-up of the quality and achievements of the 1932-33 tour, this sick question echoes with a grim relevance. It is easy to do what so many commentators have done — apologise for the fracas, attribute the signal English victory largely to the success of the intimidatory methods, and pass on in some embarrassment to the next series. Whether this is justifiable or not, it is at least understandable; there cannot be the full and pleasurable enjoyment in a victory achieved by questionable tactics, even though the answers to the questions may prove the proper exoneration of the victor. It is nevertheless easier now, fifty years later, to take a dispassionate look at the results.

Statistically, of course, the tour was a great triumph for the English party, who won ten matches and lost only the Second Test. The side stiffened in solidarity and compactness as the tour went on, (as many as eight players played in every Test,) and this led to the formation of a very powerful combination of talent, much fortified by the fact that with very few exceptions indeed everyone did themselves justice.

(The only reservations related to Maurice Tate, who was never given an adequate chance; Bill Bowes, who never reproduced his form of the 1932 season and who took only one Test wicket — but what a wicket.....; and perhaps, in Test matches, to Jardine and Ames as batsmen, although their services in their other identities, as captain and wicket-keeper respectively, were outstanding.) The confident reliability of the leading batsmen, particularly Sutcliffe and Hammond, was backed effectively by the decisive success of the bowlers — Larwood of course first, and Verity, Allen, Voce and Hammond as auxiliaries, transforming what had looked like a dangerously lop-sided attack into a combination of variety and continued menace. And every bit as deserving of mention was the sturdy range of middle-order batsmen, Leyland and Wyatt, and the disconcerting skirmisher Paynter, now, as at other times, so resourceful at need that there is cause to wonder why he was so often left out of Test sides when he succeeded so glowingly whenever he was called upon.

The truth was that English cricket was at this stage enjoying a rich period of high talent; the only imbalance, not to be righted until next season and then only temporarily, was the lack of a quite adequate opening batsman to replace Hobbs. On the other side of the fence the Australians were, for the time being, uncertain of themselves. Over the past three seasons they had relied on Bradman to supply the bulk of an unchaseable total, but this time they found that for the reasons sufficiently perceptible in the foregoing account they had to help in providing some of the essential backbone and foundation themselves, and had not quite the confidence or the technique to do it on the difficult terms presented to them. Bradman's contribution I have already tried to assess; it is enigmatic, but I think essentially was a courageous attempt to pit one kind of genius against another, in which orthodoxy had to be sacrificed along with stability. Statistically, in the Tests, he had a better average than anyone on either side except Paynter, who was helped by two not-outs in five innings; and this is the measure of his resource: that he could jettison his carefully perfected technique and play it by improvisation and still be, in his context, the master of them all. Yet he was not the master on whom his colleagues relied; and his new vulnerability destroyed their essential confidence along with his own. Jack Hobbs had the best summing-up: "I think he gave up too early. He has my sympathy."

The destructive force of Jardine's policy unsettled and unseated two of the finest Australian batsmen, Ponsford and Kippax. Ponsford was to make a satisfying recovery on the slower wickets, and against less aggressive attacks, in England in 1934; but although Kippax returned too, his clear classical freedom never regained its confident authority. There must be regret for both of these good players in that they neither appear to have had the application or the inclination to face the new menace and wear it down, as Ponsford might have, or attack it with fluency, as Kippax might have, and as McCabe, at least once, did. The Australian selectors, deprived of much of their expected strength in this way, had to rely on journeyman courage to see them through − the long-headed experienced insouciance of Victor Richardson or the youthful determination of Jack Fingleton (whom they discarded too soon.) For the rest there was the spasmodically brilliant but ultimately vaguely unreliable McCabe, and the untried and deceptively promising Darling and Bromley. There remained of the batsmen the determinedly un-shakeable Woodfull, who in the statistical matter of runs per innings troubled no computers whatever but whose stature remained for honourable acknowledgment in far higher esteem at the end of the series than his much greater numerical achievements had ever entitled him to in the past. Woodfull's obdurate resolution in the face of incalculable stresses mark him as one of Australia's great players, never mind his limited technique: but he could not serve Australia by resolution alone. His bowlers were not, at this stage, quite good enough for the England batsmen. Grimmett had lost his efficacy; Wall was steady and sometimes, as in the Adelaide Test, a most effective early weapon, but did not normally keep up his hostility as Larwood could; Ironmonger was canny and accurate but perhaps not penetrating enough; and none of the newcomers had any real effect on the powerful English batting. Only O'Reilly, in his first Test meeting with his great rivals, showed himself as entirely worthy of the tradition: and here we saw the first flexing of that most menacing genius whom Bradman has since, and there can be argument about this but no finality, called the greatest bowler in the game's history. Even so he had not the support; and had to wait for another series or two for his potentiality to be exploited to its highest degree, when by that time Fleetwood-Smith, recovering from the terrible battering strategically handed out to him by Hammond, would mature beside him as a very formidable partner indeed. For the moment, Australia had to give England best; and it is a question, which can never be settled by an conclusive

argument, whether they would have beaten England if
Jardine and Larwood had refrained from the dreaded
leg-theory technique. Without Bradman, I think Australia
would probably have lost anyway; with him, the probabilities
are so incalculable as to make it hardly worth while
discussing them. That Bradman was reduced to normal size
was the aim and the technical justification of the entire
campaign. Whether the end justified the means is another
matter altogether.

> Here were the end, had anything an end;
> Thus lit and launched, up and up roared and soared
> A rocket, till the key o' the vault was reached
> And wide heaven held, a breathless minute-space
> In brilliant usurpature........
> The act, over and ended, falls and fades:
> What was once seen, grows what is now described,
> Then talked of, told about, a tinge the less
> In every fresh transmission: till it melts,
> Trickles in silent orange or warm grey
> Across our memory, dies and leaves all dark,
> And presently we find the stars again.

It would certainly be a relief to all if one could have
dusted one's hands here and announced the end of trials and
tribulations and the resumption of normality. By the time
they all got back the spring of 1933 was maturing into a
warm bright summer, the West Indians were on the point of
joining battle, and such distresses that the winter encounters
had engendered might normally have been locked away as

past history and supplanted by constructive attention to the
matter in hand. There is no need to say that that is not the
way things happen; post-mortems were instituted without
delay; and they differed from the vast majority of post-
mortems in the crucial particular that these caused pain and
distress to the prime subjects of the operation.

The cables that had volleyed back and forth across the
globe during the winter had not unnaturally disturbed the
M.C.C.'s placid hibernation and there was little delay before
they summoned the key members of the touring party for a
first-hand account of what it had all been about. But of
necessity these deliberations took time, as well they might,
and before any of them could solidify into relevant policy
the public were treated to the first of a series of personal
revelations which, whether they can be said to have clarified
the issue or not, at least informed it with passionate intensity
all over again. This first major exploitation of what have now
unfortunately come to be called the *media* came from
Larwood himself, who, it will be remembered, had travelled
back earlier than the main body and was, in the course of
nature, met at Suez by a vast horde of newspapermen and
assorted publicists, including his county captain Arthur Carr
under contract with the *Daily Sketch*. All these accompanied
him back to London trying in vain to bribe him to break his
M.C.C. contract and spill them his full version (Carr, in fact,
although commissioned by a newspaper, being largely instrumental in seeing that the Press failed to get what they
wanted) — and after he had had practically to fight his way
yard by yard from Dover to Nottingham through hordes of
reporters shoving notebooks in his face, he sensibly kept his

mouth shut until the rest of the team arrived home in early May. Thereupon, assuming that his contract with the M.C.C. had now concluded, he authorised the publication in the *Sunday Express* of an interview with their sporting editor.

This interview did no more than put into fairly straight language Larwood's committed opinion that the controversial form of attack was justifiable, that the Australian Press and public had made far too much row about it, that the behaviour of the crowds had been outrageous, and that the main causes for the vociferous complaints were that Woodfull was too slow to combat this attack successfully and (here comes the crucial point) Bradman too frightened. And it is not surprising that this last unequivocal statement was the one that called forth the most forceful disagreement. Bradman for one, and I cannot see that he is to be blamed for this, resented rather warmly the imputation that he was scared; many other Australians, as might have been expected, shared his resentment and said so. From among them may be singled out in particular Arthur Mailey, whose dispatches from the actual field of battle had been conspicuous throughout the campaign for their temperate fair-mindedness; in one of the more balanced of Australian reactions he admitted that many of Larwood's comments were reasonable but said that his criticisms of Woodfull and Bradman were definately unfair. The Australian Press broke out into a general babel of commentary and accusation, and were answered across the globe by its equally energetic but perhaps less authoritatively informed British counterpart. Most of Larwood's fellow-players on the touring party were canny enough to maintain a discreet silence, however pertinaciously the Press flocked round them for anything they had to offer; and even Jardine confined himself for the present to a long article in a provincial paper (the *Nottingham Evening News*) in which he predictably defended himself with clarity and dignity, deplored the attitude of the Australian Board of Control, particularly in respect of their inability to exercise authority over the behaviour of their crowds, and finally paid tribute to the loyalty of his team. Unexceptionable indeed; but in no sense approaching the heart of the matter. It was perhaps too early to expect anyone to be able to do this effectively, yet; but clearly it was not long before efforts were going to be made, and very soon indeed it was announced that full-length apologias were in preparation, one by Larwood himself and another by Jardine. (And of course it must be understood that when I say "by Larwood himself" I mean "by an anonymous journalist, Larwood getting the credit and presumably most of the money". The authorship of Jardine's book I would feel to be more doubtful. Jardine, an educated and highly articulate man, would not normally need a ghost-writer; but it is difficult to trace, in the characterless prose of the book eventually published, the distinctive style and wit which one would expect to inform any considered self-expression of the Jardine whom we have grown to know.)

Both these books, then, were in busy preparation in the summer of 1933; and at the same time the M.C.C. got down to examining the reports from the tour managers and to trying to get to grips with the elusive truth. The managers, Warner and Palairet, were of course called into council, together with Jardine, and they all appeared in due course

before a sub-committee specifically appointed to investigate
the whole body-line affair. Larwood records that he was not
invited, and there is evidence that the selection of interested
parties to testify before the sub-committee was not a very
wide one, and that it is possible that the M.C.C. were not
officially favoured with all varieties of informed opinion. It
follows that it may have taken longer for the authorities in
England to become conversant with the whole subject in the
round, as it were, than the much-maligned Australian Board
of Control would have liked; and the reactions from this side
of the world were in consequence slow to show themselves.
What did appear, quite unequivocally and quite soon,
however, was that Warner expressed himself, now that he was
back home, as firmly opposed to the practice of leg-theory,
just as he been last summer before he left.

Meanwhile the Australian Board of Control had done
some positive work; and as early as 21 April 1933 they had,
with commendable practical sense, formulated a proposed
addition to the existing Laws of Cricket in Australia which
they accordingly forwarded a week later to the M.C.C. at
Lord's for consideration and approval; the first serious
attempt to resolve a difficult and still indeterminate
situation.

"The Australian Board ...", they said, "have adopted
following addition to Laws of Cricket in Australia, namely:—

"Any ball delivered which in the opinion of the umpire at
the bowler's end is bowled at the batsman with the intent to
intimidate or injure him shall be considered unfair, and "No
Ball" shall be called. The bowler shall be notified of the

reason. If the offence be repeated by the same bowler in the same innings he shall be immediately instructed by the umpire to cease bowling and the over shall be regarded as completed. Such bowler shall not again be permitted to bowl during the course of the innings then in progress.....

"Foregoing submitted for your consideration and it is hoped co-operation by application to all cricket."

The M.C.C., upon receipt of the foregoing so submitted, sat upon it for six weeks, during which they completed their interrogation of such members of the touring party whom they wished to interview, and considered all the reports. They then concocted a long reply, which I do not propose to set out in full here, but of which it is sufficient to say that it made four main points.

First: The M.C.C., recording their assumption that the class of bowling referred to in the proposal was that referred to in a previous cable as "Body-line", registered a powerful objection to the implications of the term. They said that it was misleading and improper and had led to much inaccuracy of thought by confusing the short, bumping ball whether directed on the off, middle or leg stump, with what is known as "leg-theory". They went on to say that the term 'body-line' would appear to imply a direct attack by the bowler on the batsman, and they emphatically proclaimed their view that such an implication applied to any English bowling in Australia was improper and incorrect. They went on to say that the practice of bowling on the leg stump with a field set on the leg side was legitimate and had been in force for many years.

Second: They regarded the proposed new Law as impracticable. Firstly, they said, it would place an impossible task on the umpire, and secondly, it would place in the hands of the umpire a power over the game which would be more than dangerous, and which any umpire might well fear to exercise.

Third: They would watch carefully during the present season for anything which might be regarded as unfair or prejudicial to the best interests of the game, and would invite opinions of county clubs and captains at the end of the season. They spoke of a special meeting of the Imperial Cricket Conference at which all these opinions could be co-ordinated and discussed.

Fourth: They then carried the war into the enemy's country and made a full-blooded complaint about the objectionable nature of the barracking in Australia. They minced no words about this, and ended with ominous noises – "little or no effort on the part of those responsible to control this exhibition ... serious lack of consideration for members of the team ... the Committee are of opinion that cricket played under such conditions is robbed of much of its value as a game... unless barracking is stopped or is greatly moderated in Australia, it is difficult to see how the continuance of representative matches can serve the best interest of the game."

And with this very nasty veiled threat, the missive concluded, winding up with a formal but reasonable regret that these matters had to be dealt with by correspondence and not by personal conference – a difficulty that air travel has by now largely surmounted.

It is perhaps a pity that a point could not have been stretched, and an emissary sent to Lord's from Australia at once. A first-hand account from someone in the opposite camp — or, not to put too fine a point upon it, at the other end of the pitch — might have been more immediately persuasive and convincing than the most conscientiously forbearing of cablegrams, and might have saved time, trouble and heartburn and avoided the year-long drag of painful diplomatic negotiation. As it is, it was September before the Australians were able to concoct a full reply to the M.C.C.'s broadside; and by that time another cricket season in England was virtually over.

During that cricket season a number of isolated developments occurred, it can fairly be said, independently of each other, but all stemming from the central situation of which everybody was still painfully and unavoidably aware, whether it was openly discussed as a living issue or not. Quite an appreciable number of leading fast bowlers bowled some form of leg-theory or other up and down the county championship; Larwood took very little part because of his injury, but Voce used it frequently and so did Bill Bowes and Clark of Northants. Ken Farnes, then an up-and-coming Cambridge Blue of promise, electrified the Establishment by employing the technique in the University Match, and effectively too, for he was fast and accurate; several batsmen were hit on the body and at least two were dismissed when the ball rose sharply and hit them on the neck, causing them to stumble on to their wickets. Not a great deal of publicity attended upon these comparatively mild symptoms, though there were murmurings up and down the country at Bowes' habit of pitching short and sharp not once but sometimes three or four times an over; but such inheritances from the previous winter as can be said to hold any historical significance in the story of this menacing tactic are to be traced not so much in the comparatively undisturbed progress of the domestic game but in the rather more vigorous and independent activities of the international visitors for the season, the West Indies. These happy and maturing cricketers, not yet quite in the top class but coming up strongly, had with them one supreme fast bowler, E.A. Martindale, a light, rangy, whippy performer with turned-in toes and a lovely action. His companions in speed for the greater part of the tour were not his measure in quality or in menance of attack: but for the very few matches for which he could be released from his contract with his club in the Lancashire League, Learie Constantine was able to join him; and these two constituted the fastest pair of openers since Gregory and McDonald, if one has to grant that the combined speeds of Larwood and Voce, or Larwood and Allen, did not quite reach theirs. This double barrage was loosed upon the waiting world for the first time on the occasion of the match between the tourists and the M.C.C. at Lord's in late May; when the M.C.C. opening batsmen, coming in to face the last hour or so of the first day's play after the West Indies had been put out for 309, were submitted to a rather fierce bombardment which they found it a disconcerting business to weather. These two bowlers bowled very fast indeed, and they served up a startling proportion of bouncers; and although they did not pack the leg-field obtrusively it seemed that most of the bowling that evening was directed if not at the batsmen then let us say in the area of the leg stump or thereabouts. The opening batsmen, neither of them exclusively specialist in that position, were Jack Hearne and Joe Hulme, the first of them aged 42 and a little past his best and the other an excellent middle-order campaigner with comparatively limited experience of new-ball attack. I was there, and my heart bled for them both as these limber West Indians, bounding springily up to the wicket in the evening light after a day's restful contemplation (neither had done more in the batting line than enjoy a short cheerful bash), whistled it again and again round their startled ears. Hulme twice to my recollection had his bat knocked out of his hands as he fended off neck-high bouncers, and once he nearly fell on his wicket. Hearne, instinct as always with a characteristic quiet dignity that never deserted him, was late on his stroke several times, collected the odd bruise in the ribs with studied calm, but was clearly unsettled and unwontedly tentative. They stuck to it manfully enough, and they scored a run or two here and a run or two there: but I do not think that I am maligning a great player when I say that after a time Hearne had clearly had enough and that in so far as it was consistent with his unshakeable decorum and sense of duty he patently if not blatantly gave his wicket away. He swished under a bouncer and offered a skier to the wicket-keeper: and I have rarely seen a batsman more contented and relieved to get out. (In the next match he played he made 93 against Voce: may I hereby re-establish his reputation.) Another wicket or two went down that night, but not Hulme's, who had the week-end to contemplate the re-mounting of the attack on

Monday, when nobody lasted very long anyway except Brian Valentine and the erratic Chapman, who chanced his arm and only missed a hundred by three runs. As a postscript to this rather bizarre episode it should perhaps be added that among the M.C.C. batsmen who failed before Constantine and Martindale during their first innings (when they shared all the wickets but one) was one D.R. Jardine, who however was one of only two batsmen to make a decent score in the second. And as a post-postscript it might also be said that the West Indies may have in the upshot wondered whether their tactics might not have in part recoiled on their own head when Bill Bowes, who was in the M.C.C. side on this occasion, bumped one at their best batsman, George Headley, in the second innings, hit him on the chest, and kept him out of the side for the next three matches.

This particular exercise might possibly be regarded as a high-spirited eccentricity: no protest was made beyond a few vociferated comments from the crowd, as in sober fact this kind of thing was what they had been watching Bowes do for a season or more, and the prime difference in the immediate circumstances was that the West Indian bowlers were two and not one and bowled on a general computation half as fast again as he did. The West Indians themselves made no consistent practice of these bouncers (partly, no doubt, because of the general non-availability of Constantine) but they did not lose sight of their potentialities in this direction, and staged what is now a classic confrontation during the Second Test Match at Old Trafford at the end of July.

The first Test at Lord's in June was badly affected by rain and was won rather easily by England, whose spinners caught the West Indies on a treacherous wicket and found them with little resource to defend themselves. Manchester, however, offered, by way of a change, a true hard wicket for which both sides had batting talent and to spare, and the spinners were ineffective until the last day of all, when it was too late to save the match from a foregone draw. None of the fast bowlers who had toured Australia were in the England side — Larwood's foot had still not recovered, Voce had gone stale as a result of his heavy winter's work, Allen was not available (he only played in two first-class matches that season), and Bowes at that point was suffering from an injury; and the chief spearhead of the England attack was Clark of Northants. Jardine was of course still captain: but there is no record that he made use of the leg-theory technique in the West Indies first innings even though, after winning the toss, they scored 333 for six on the first day, materially assisted by a fine second-wicket stand by Headley and the wicket-keeper Barrow, who got a century each and added exactly 200. The total eventually reached 375; and it was when England began on their reply that Constantine and Martindale reverted to the tactic which they had already tried out briefly but cheerfully at Lord's.

The Australians, far away in the depths of winter, must have chuckled with delight when they read about it; for Constantine and Martindale turned on all the speed they had, crowded the leg side and as nearly as possible provided for the Manchester crowd a faithful version of what the discomposed Australians had had to face six months before on the other side of the world. The two fast bowlers treated the English batsmen to a prolonged barrage of fliers and kickers, and whatever the batsmen may have felt about it, it was made fairly clear that the crowd cared for it very little and the critics even less. And as for the batsmen, one in particular is reported to have expressed an adverse opinion — Hammond, who took a rearing bouncer on the chin and had to retire for treatment. When he returned he soon received a duplicate delivery which he got his bat to in self-defence and was caught in the leg-trap; which according to reports led to a repetition of his earlier comment that if this was what Test cricket was coming to, the quicker he gave it up the better. Without capsizing the head and middle of the English batting, it appreciably discomposed it, and four formidable wickets went down for 134 — a further quick success and the struggle could have been a desperate one. It is almost superfluous, but it is at the same time fitting and satisfying to record, that the batsman to stand four-square against this alarming attack was Jardine. Justice must be preserved; he was not the only one, and Ames and Robins are entitled to very considerable credit too, helping him as they did with vitally constructive stands of 83 and 140, by which time the fire was dying and the venom exhausted. But it is right and proper that Jardine, who to all present intents and purposes was the inventor of this baleful form of aggression, and was quite clearly designed by the spirited West Indians to be the chief recipient of their particularly vivid version of it, should go down in cricketing history as the batsman who displayed in full and convincing detail the correct way in which it could be faced and, with care and application, defeated. McCabe in the first Sydney Test had offered one recipe, gallant, resourceful, effective, but I suppose in the long run dangerous; Jardine here demonstrated a complementary version. McCabe had trusted to eye and timing and lightning footwork for an all-out policy of attack; he had batted for four hours, made 187 not out and hit 25 boundaries. Jardine, trusting as naturally to eye and timing and footwork, used these almost entirely in highly skilled and impeccably organised defence; he made his tallness even taller, playing the fierce risers again and again down on to the wicket from a dead bat classically straight; he was in for five hours, made 127 and hit five fours. As was customary with him he ignored hits on the body, being seemingly constructed of leather and gristle; and never allowed near misses to the head and face to discompose his concentration, which was at all times of an unshakeable intensity. As an innings it was masterly, as a gesture it was superbly appropriate, as the climax to a prolonged dramatic action it could not have been surpassed. It was the only century that he ever made in a Test, and there can be no doubt that he would have given his ears to have been able to make it against Australia. This innings hoisted the England total to within a single run of their opponents; Clark tried some leg-theory again in the second innings without much success, the ultimate spinners' breakthrough was delayed too long to be of real value, and the match was left drawn. Jardine was unhappily prevented from continuing the campaign into the third and last Test at the Oval by an injury which he collected in a subsequent county match; his successor as captain, Wyatt, was not the man to exploit leg-theory even if he had had the bowlers to use it effectively, and Constantine was not available for the tourists, so although the match was easily won by England, it had no relevance to the theme so challengingly stated by the West Indians at Lord's and Old Trafford.

There is no doubt, however, that its exploitation by these bowlers in front of English witnesses had been of great value. It could perhaps be argued that even granted the vivid talents of Constantine and Martindale the brand of leg-theory served up was not of the potency that Jardine had been able to command when Larwood was fully fit. (It would have been interesting to see Jardine himself batting for Surrey against Larwood and Voce bowling for Notts. on a fast-paced Oval wicket and employing authentic leg-theory: but it was not to be.) Nevertheless what the English spectators saw of it was sufficient to make them take thought; and if the editor of *Wisden* can be regarded as in any true sense representative of them, we are assured that the thoughts they had about it were less than exhilarating. "The fact that Jardine showed that it was possible to meet it without suffering physical injury or losing his wicket through any impatient or wild stroke" — so his account of the Old Trafford Test runs — "did not make the sight of (the fast leg-theory bowling) any more welcome, and most of those who were watching it for the first time must have come to the conclusion that, while strictly within the law, it was not nice." (Lovely phrase.)

It was after the end of the season in which these stirring versions of distant battles had been enacted before the very eyes of the game's chief legislators that the Australian Board of Control enunciated their reply to the three-month-old cable in which the M.C.C. had spread itself and spoken with a certain peremptoriness in its voice. And in this reply comes loud and clear between the lines the reminder that next season, 1934, was due to display as its centrepiece the visit of Australia to England, where, in case somebody did something about it and did it sharpish, all would be to do again. They accordingly fell back in this cable of 22 September into what might be called a new conciliatory tone.

"We note you consider", the message ran, "that a form of bowling which amounted to a direct attack on the batsman would be against the spirit of the game. We agree with you that leg-theory bowling as it has been generally practised for many years is not open to objection. On these matters there does not appear to be any real difference between our respective views.

We feel that while the type of bowling to which exception was taken in Australia was not strictly in conflict with the Laws of Cricket yet its continued practice would not be in the best interests of the game. May we assume that you concur in this point of view and that the teams may thus take the field in 1934 with that knowledge?

We are giving consideration to the question of barracking and you may rely upon our using our best endeavours to have it controlled in future tours.

We are most anxious that the cordial relations which have so long existed between English and Australian cricket shall continue."

Unexceptionable sentiments; with certain interesting emphases in the second paragraph — one, a sturdy adherence to the original Australian grievance: two, a further turn in the persuasive screw by those who were determined, even if it

took them years, to force the M.C.C. to a plain acknowledgment of what seemed to the Australians plain obvious:
three, anxiety about the imminent tour of England. One does
not need to desert what one intends as a sedulous impart-
iality to express a genuine admiration for their dogged
persistence. The M.C.C. administrators, whether they ad-
mired it or not, had once more to bend their diplomatic
minds to produce what might be interpreted as a convincing
answer, and it is clear that they took some trouble to do so,
as well as an equal amount of trouble to avoid committing
themselves to what they had been specifically asked to
commit themselves to. They stated in their reply of 9
October:—

"In the view of the Committee, the difference between us
seems to be rather on the question of fact than on any point
of interpretation of the Laws of Cricket or of the spirit of the
game. They agree and have always agreed that a form of
bowling which is obviously a direct attack by the bowler
upon the batsman would be an offence against the spirit of
the game.

Your team can certainly take the field with the knowledge and with the full assurance that cricket will be played
here in the same spirit as in the past and with the single desire
to promote the best interests of the game in both countries."

And after an approving acknowledgment of the Australian promise to review the barracking question, they
concluded:

"Your team can rely on a warm welcome from M.C.C.,
and every effort will be made to make their visit enjoyable."

It may be felt that the Australian spokesmen, who were in fact under considerable pressure from their own side, players and administrators alike, to get their prime preoccupation properly discussed and their serious objection honestly confronted and answered by the M.C.C., could have been less than satisfied with that last missive which answered no direct question but merely reiterated general goodwill and nailed nobody to anything. Whatever they said or felt in private, they took time to ruminate before making their reactions public. For this, that and the other reason it was a month before they could frame their reply; and when it was set out on 16 November it was laconic.

"We appreciate the terms of your cablegram of October 9 and assume that such cable is intended to give the assurance asked for in our cablegram of September 22.

It is on this understanding that we are sending a team in 1934."

There is a pointed directness about this cable (which also, it is to be presumed, had the virtue of being considerably less expensive than the average run of this correspondence) which cannot have been lost upon the administrators at Lord's, who may have been chary of the straight statement but who no doubt knew a straight hint when they saw one. It could not have been stated more plainly that when the Australians *said* that they assumed that the previous cable was intended to give the required assurance they actually *meant* that it was quite clear to them that it was intended emphatically to avoid doing just that. The concluding sentence was also, equally plainly, intended to be taken as meaning what it said. If they were satisfied that the required assurance was forthcoming they would readily proceed with the projected tour. If on the other hand they were not so satisfied, they would not. And however complaisantly the first paragraph of their cable might read, the tone and design of the entire communication made it clear to the meanest intelligence that they were not satisfied yet.

The M.C.C. delayed their reply for nearly another month. In the meantime, on 23 November, a joint meeting of the Advisory County Cricket Committee and the Board of Control of Test Matches at Home took place at Lord's to concern itself with the proposal put up months ago by the Australians for the insertion of the new law against fast leg-theory bowling. All the counties had been circularised: all the counties were represented at the meeting. It is no surprise to learn that it was decided after due deliberation that no alteration of the laws was desirable. An agreement was formulated, on the lines pursued all through the cable-correspondence, that any form of direct attack by bowler against batsman would be an offence against the spirit of the game; and it was decided to leave the whole matter in the hands of the captains in complete confidence that they would not permit or countenance bowling of such type.

It certainly appears that at this time there was a very serious possibility of the 1934 tour of England by an Australian team being cancelled because the Australians were not confident that this tactic, to which the majority of them were utterly opposed, would not be used upon them again. The M.C.C., however hard they were pressed, were proving predictably niggardly of concessions; and it appears that round about this stage of the proceedings a great deal of backstairs negotiations and discussion was going on, and that the cablegrams were only the outward and visible signs of busy diplomatic activity. By this time the Australian Board of Control had at least one representative, if not more, in constant negotiation with M.C.C. sub-committees — and there have been hints that he conveyed verbally some suggestion that if England used body-line in the forthcoming series Australia would use it too — which failed to shake the M.C.C. Committee. It was also at this stage or thereabouts that sombre fears that a rift between the two cricketing fraternities might seriously affect the loyal political relationships between the Mother Country and her illustrious Dominion caused an extension of activity behind the scenes from St. John's Wood as far as Whitehall, where the buck travelled as far as the Secretary for the Dominions, the Right Hon. J.H. Thomas himself. A less congruous figure in this particularized context it would be hard to call to the imagination, but the incongruity is less significant than the approach to him. (It is possible that the apparent extravagance of the manoeuvre may be partly discounted by the fact that the then President of the M.C.C., Lord Hailsham, was himself a Cabinet Minister at the time, and that the approach was a less unnatural move than it might otherwise have seemed. And it is also apparent from the records that valuable conciliatory work was done by Sir Alexander Hore-Ruthven, Governor of South Australia, who briefed the Dominions Secretary on the state of Australian public opinion.)

Whatever may have been going on behind whatever illustrious doors, the M.C.C. were ready in December with their reply to the importunate Australian cable; and the tone of their communication carried with it a sharp tang of frost. It was dated 12 December.

"Reference your cable of November 16th", it began, and if that didn't put them off for a start I do not know what would, "you must please accept our cable of October 9th, which speaks for itself, as final.

We cannot go beyond the assurance therein given. We shall welcome Australian cricketers who come to play cricket with us next year. If, however, your Board of Control decide that such games should be deferred, we shall regret their decision.

Please let us know your Board's final decision as soon as possible, and in any event before the end of the year."

This little billet carried with it an authoritarian abruptness that communicated itself without any delay whatever to the Australian recipients. Their reply came back two days later, abandoning all defiance. For one reason or another, and after what pressure from without or within is not known, they acquiesced at once.

"With further reference to your cable of October 9", they wired on 14 December, "and your confirmatory cable of December 12 in reply to ours of November 16, we, too, now regard the position as finalised. Our team will leave Australia on March 9."

We can picture the relief and satisfaction at Lord's — a rigid policy of deflection and stonewalling had broken the spirit of the attack. It has been suggested that the hurried capitulation of the Australians was by no means a unanimous one and that the decision to take the line they did was reached by a narrow majority in the absence of some of the Board's members. Nevertheless, by whatever means, the danger of a major disaster had been averted; and whether one can necessarily sympathise completely with the evasive tactics of the M.C.C. or dissociate oneself entirely from the indignant pertinacity of the Australians, it can be surely agreed that it was better for the series to continue with cracks rather obviously papered over than for a formal rift in England-Australia cricketing relationships to be registered.

"Thank you for your cable," said the M.C.C. on the very same date, 14 December, "We are very glad to know we may look forward to welcoming the Australians next summer. We shall do all in our power to make their visit enjoyable."

And then everyone drew a long breath and relaxed. And if it had been quite as simple as that, it may be that wounds would have healed quicker; but it wasn't. It was not long before the M.C.C. had to take serious thought in the direction of the implementation of the promise contained in the last sentence of the last cable; and would have to consider not only what to do to make the Australian visit enjoyable: but also, quite specifically, what not to do.

Jardine, who quite naturally and predictably had continued to defend his practice without the smallest reservation, was not a close party to these winter activities, for the very good reason that the M.C.C. had appointed him captain of the touring side due to visit India. It is clear enough that they had appointed him because on present record he was by far the best captain available and there was no real doubt, even when his comparatively mediocre performance in Australia was taken into account, that his capacity as a batsman still put him very high up in the English ranks. (If any evidence was needed, his innings at Old Trafford was surely sufficient.) It must also be clear that his reappointment after the doubts and dangers of the winter was also a positive re-statement by the M.C.C. of their continued faith in him, and of their tacit endorsement of his right to pursue what policies he thought fit. As a result of this appointment, he was personally too far away from the consultations that went on during the winter to be able to offer advice, remonstrance, exhortation or what he would; but the signs begin to point without much doubt towards a swing in official favour taking effect during the winter of 1933-34. Not away from Jardine as a cricketer and a captain: but away from his policy, which whether they were ever disposed to agree with it or not, must be allowed to have caused them, over the past twelve months or so, unprecedented embarrassment.

Jardine, for his part, may have sensed that the tide of opinion in authoritative circles was turning against his own firmly-held views. He had spent much of the summer preparing his own book on the Australian tour and had had plenty of opportunity to review and consolidate his own conclusions; on the Indian tour the 'body-line' techniques were, so far as can be seen, not used to any extent, though Clark and Nichols, the two fast bowlers, were reported to have made the ball fly from time to time, but not of elaborate design. His self-communication during the long months did, however, bring him to the point where the contemplation of an imminent Australian tour of England was too much for him: and towards the end of the Indian venture he made, and allowed to be published, the unequivocal declaration that he had neither the desire nor the intention of playing against the Australians during the coming summer; which had the virtue, at least, of making his attitude absolutely clear, and of removing from the plates of the Selection Committee a very ticklish and embarrassing problem indeed. It also removed from Test cricket (and virtually, as it turned out, from first class cricket altogether, since his resignation from the captaincy of Surrey was announced at about the same time) one of the most accomplished of all performers at an age where as the custom used to run in those days there must have been nearly ten years of good cricket in him.

With the problem of Jardine neatly, if not really very happily, solved, the possibility of the M.C.C. being able to guarantee the Australians the enjoyable tour that they had promised them became a little more easy to fulfil; but there were still one or two important factors that they knew well enough that they would have to take into account. And the greatest of these was Larwood.

This bowler had spent the season of 1933 in a kind of unreal limbo, occasioned very largely by the injury to his foot, a belated operation on which reduced the number of his county appearances to twelve out of the full list of twenty-eight. Moreover, after the first two matches it was decided that he had better not bowl, so his total bag of wickets for 1933 was one for 18. (It speaks well for Nottinghamshire faith in his batting capacity that they were happy to include him in the side for his run-getting capacity alone, and he responded very well with nearly 400 runs in 18 innings.) However, the winter of 1933-34 gave him plenty of chances to recuperate, and the next (fateful) season approached with no attendant indication that his physical capacities would not be back to normal. This may have been so, with the reservations that will later have to be chronicled; but it is clear enough that well before the Australians were due to arrive he had been for one reason and another induced into a state of mind in which it was going to be very difficult to persuade him to accede to any proposition that he could not immediately accept.

Arthur Carr his captain had been one of the county representatives at Lord's in the November of 1933 when the agreement had been reached (not unanimously, and Carr was said to be one of those against the form in which it was set out, but it had been reached) that any form of fast leg-theory bowling which was obviously a direct attack upon the batsman would be contrary to the spirit of the game. It had been decided, it will be remembered, to leave the whole affair in the hands of the captains in full confidence that they would not permit or countenance bowling of this type. All of which was unexceptionable, but very naturally left each captain with the responsibility of forming his own opinion on what was or was not a direct attack on the batsman; and Carr was not very long about making it known that while he fully agreed that a direct attack, etc., was contrary to the spirit of the game, he refused to admit that leg-theory as bowled by Larwood and Voce under his direction was in fact direct attack. An opinion, of course, to which he was fully entitled; and similarly an opinion with which his opponents were equally entitled to disagree.

It should perhaps be emphasised that Larwood and Voce (1934-style under Carr in England) were perhaps not quite the fierce proposition presented by Larwood and Voce (1932-33-style under Jardine in Australia.) The English wickets, as always when these comparisons become relevant, were appreciably slower and less dangerous; Voce, even at his best, which was excellent, was never so fast or so accurate as Larwood; and Larwood of 1934 never attained, even when his foot was more or less recovered, to the terrifying speeds achieved by the Larwood of 1932-33. Nor was Carr, determined aggressor as he was, ever quite the dedicated and implacable avenger into which Jardine had determinedly moulded himself. Nevertheless, the continuance of the practice was likely to cause difficulties; which it did.

Larwood under Carr's leadership began once again to bowl with much of his old consistency and accuracy. His pace was for the future considerably modified, as the foot injury never ceased to affect it slightly; but his command of length and direction was hardly impaired at all. A vague legend has formed itself that after the notorious tour he faded at once into nothingness. This is quite untrue – in 1934 he took 82 wickets in the season at an average of 17, in 1935 102 at an average of 22, and in 1936 119 for 12 each, and was top of the first-class bowling averages. This was no fade-out: it was only in 1937 that injuries and strains began to have serious effects, which finally eased him out in 1938; so purely on figures and results his career can be said to have continued with considerable success until 1936 at least, when he was nearly thirty-two anyway, an age beyond which very few great fast bowlers have been able to maintain their greatness.

But it is not Larwood's skill or his continued use of it that is in question. And I must hasten to add to that preliminary sentence the corollary that neither his loyalty nor, I think, his temperamental self-control, are in question either. Perhaps in what followed his judgment may have been unhappily at fault; but it is difficult to see how someone in his position, subject to fierce pressures to which most of us can have no equivalent experience to match ourselves by, can lightly be criticized. The conciliatory flurries engaged in by the various representatives of the M.C.C. were of course not enterprises of a kind that they would be likely to consult him about; and early in the 1934 season he began to get an inkling that his name was being bandied about behind his back. Well, of course it was, and it would have been very unnatural if it was not: but an early intimation of it was adminstered to him when he was advised through the influential Sir Julien Cahn that it would be an advantage to his Test future if he would apologise to the M.C.C. When he asked what he was supposed to apologise for, he was told that if he apologised for bowling leg-theory and undertook not to do it again he would be considered for the Tests. If he didn't he wouldn't, and there the matter rested. This apology he flatly refused to offer: and it was not long after this that he made the decision that in effect he would not wait for the selectors to drop him, but would preserve his independence and publicly drop himself. Before he had arrived at this stage he had temporised with the situation by reporting to his county, just before the selection for the first Test was made, that he was not a hundred per cent fit. This, he confessed afterwards, was a kind of effort at self-protection, (he did not want to play but did not want not to be invited to, a recognizable condition of mind which can perhaps attract legitimate sympathy without necessarily calling for whole-hearted approval.) True enough he was omitted from the first Test, but the next few days brought him no alleviation of his doubts: and on the day that the team for the Second Test at Lord's was to be chosen he authorised the publication of an article in the *Sunday Dispatch,* in which he stated finally that he had definitely made up his mind not to play against Australia in the forthcoming Test or any other. (Plum Warner, writing many years later, revealed that had Larwood's statement not been published that day he would have been among those to whom invitations were issued.)

It is putting it mildly to say that this was a pity; the only logic to which it answers is the logic of Larwood's own temperamental inclinations which, I have already taken care to emphasise, had been for the past eighteen months or so subjected to unwarrantable and unprecedented strains. There is no reason to suppose, Jardine as captain being now *hors concours*, that he would have been required to bowl leg-theory in a Test match; and it seems clear that as Carr, even, was not asking him to do it for Notts, (having decided that Larwood's straight off-theory deliveries were sufficiently efficacious and that Voce was the bowler whom he would

require to concentrate on the leg-side techniques) there was
not going to be the remotest likelihood that these controversial manoeuvres were ever going to involve him again. Even
so, Larwood chose to veto his own selection: depriving
England of its best fast bowler once and for all — for even at
a reduced pace he was still the finest of them all. (I would
not insert this following hint had he himself not voiced it in
his own book: but the feeling at the back of his mind that on
English wickets and without high-pressure leg-theory he
could no longer expect to master Bradman, who had so
signally dominated him four years before, may have had a
cogent influence on his final determination. Even in temporary eclipse the potency of Bradman proved to be
decisive.)

It was at precisely this time, when tempers in Nottinghamshire must have been bubbling dangerously near to the
lid of the pot, unbeknown to us all in our innocence, that
Lancashire, engaged in a county match at Trent Bridge,
endured three days of assault and battery which can only
have been the result of a communal explosion of resentment
against the world in general. Lancashire, never a county to
suffer in respectful silence, objected vociferously to being
subjected to retaliation down the leg side for something
which was not their fault; their quarrel was not so much with
Larwood's destructiveness in the first innings — he took six
for 51, having at one time taken all six in five overs for one
run only, and what is more had five catches dropped off him
— but with the ill-tempered tactics in the second innings.
Larwood was by this time a little less effective, (having
worked off a good deal of his bad blood by making 80 in

three-quarters of an hour) but Voce was particularly aggressive in his exploitation of the leg-theory techniques and the Lancashire batsmen took a heavy battering. (Ironically it was quite useless: they. made 394 for seven and went on to win the match; but their batsmen were black and blue, and so was their recriminatory language — George Duckworth in particular, who had, as it were, befriended Larwood in Australia and defended body-line back home, taking a slightly less than deserved bruising in his capacity as a Lancashire batsman and in consequence severely modifying his commendations of the tactic.) As a result of this, sharp words passed between the two counties, and Lancashire preferred not to arrange a fixture with Nottinghamshire for the following season.

Much later in the season another county felt that it had occasion to protest; this was Middlesex, whose late order batsmen found themselves at the wrong end of a concentrated assault by Voce, who hit several of them while bowling fast leg-theory and caused one of them to retire not only hurt but unconscious. Again angry correspondence threatened relations between the counties: this time a conciliatory reply by Nottinghamshire prevented a public breach. Nevertheless there can be no doubt that Nottinghamshire cricket found itself seriously disturbed and disrupted by the events and the processes that had led up to them; but by neither of these county controversies to anything like the extent that was effected by the maladministration of the match at Trent Bridge between the county and the touring Australian team, which took place late in the tour on 11th August, shortly before the last Test.

By the time that this match was played, Carr was no longer in daily command of the team. He was of course the offical captain, and had been in full charge during the Lancashire match of doubtful fame; but a few weeks later he had been visited with sudden illness — in fact, a mild heart attack, and for the rest of the season he was not fit to play. (He made, as it happens, a good recovery, and was fully prepared to resume for the following season.) As a result the captaincy was entrusted in the emergency to Ben Lilley, the wicket-keeper and senior professional; and it was under his supervision, although nobody appears to accuse him of personal responsibility for any of it, that the trouble with Middlesex, and more particularly the trouble with the Australians, occurred.

The Australians at Trent Bridge were facing Bill Voce for the first time on the tour, Larwood of course keeping his promise and staying away; and after Woodfull and Bill Brown had put up 70 for the first wicket when they had won the toss, the rest all found themselves in considerable discomfort with the short-pitched deliveries with which the left-hander was favouring them, assisted in his war of nerves by five fielders on the leg side, four of them with their hot breath on the back of the batsman's neck. Only Woodfull and Chipperfield played him with any confidence; it would seem beyond question that additional venom was imparted into Voce's aggression by a feeling, whoever may have induced it, that Larwood had not been fairly treated; and although the Australian total could be called respectable (it was 237) it was smaller than their average expectations and Voce took 8 for 66 in 23 overs. (Bradman, it should be noted, was not playing.) The Australians, unsettled by this onslaught and by bursts of the very much less than friendly barracking with which the Notts crowd accompanied it, redeemed their *amour propre* by dismissing the county's admirable batting side for only 183. There was time for only four overs on the second evening for the Australians to begin their reply: two of which were bowled by Voce with such patent hostility that action was thereafter taken in the Australian camp. There was a great deal of hurried and peremptory diplomatic activity between the county and their discomposed visitors; as a consequence of which the Australians bluntly declared that if Voce went into the field against them the next morning they would withdraw from the match.

Confronted with this frightful possibility (for in the context of international cricket it *was* frightful, and the Australians knew what they were doing) Nottinghamshire capitulated, and resorted to the subterfuge of instructing Voce, who had never felt fitter in his life, to report sick. Whether he did this, or whether to save embarrassment and trouble, it was done for him, is not stated — what we do know is that he was unable to take his place in the field that day as he was suffering from sore shins. Whereupon the Australians made 230 for two and managed an easy draw, being subjected, on taking the field for the last innings, to some violently abusive barracking which left them in no doubt as to whose side the Trent Bridge spectators were on.

As a result of this incident and the accumulations of stress and strain that had preceded and were to follow it, the Notts County Cricket Club entered upon a crowded period of hasty activity. Cumbered with protests from Australia,

Middlesex and Lancashire, and, if hints are to be believed, threats of further protests from numerous other first-class counties as well, with the attractive prospect of a depleted fixture list next year and hardly any fixtures at all the year after, they called committee after committee and meeting after meeting. At long last, after several months of apology, uncertainty and what can only be surmised to be intrigue, they informed Carr three days before Christmas, by way of a seasonable message of goodwill and statement of pleasure in his recovery, that he was no longer captain and that the leadership had (to make the blow harder) been offered to two joint captains for next season.

The justice of this action seems dubious. Carr's fifteen years of outstanding service as captain of the county, his own brilliant and forthright abilities, his sterling backing of his own professionals — added to the undoubted fact that he could by no chance whatever have been regarded as personally responsible for what had occurred in the latter half of the recent season: all this balanced against his undoubtedly injudicious and sometimes rebellious attitude to authority, particularly on the recent delicate topic, and of course his own sometimes headstrong and perhaps quarrelsome nature — all this resolved in a blink by a cool removal, notified to him according to his own account by the public Press before he ever received a letter, formal or otherwise. How often we find a county club, with reason perhaps on its side, counteracting its own honourable purpose by the thoughtless ineptitude of the process by which it seeks to enforce it. Carr in his disjointed book, *Cricket With the Lid Off*, gives a long account of the enormous protest meeting of his well-wishers summoned immediately after the news of his deposition and including a message from Voce declaring that the "sore shins" business was a pure invention, roars of applause and uncounted encomiums for Carr, a warming and encouraging occasion no doubt, but doing nobody any good at all. Had he not specifically stated in his book for some reason or other that he had never sat out a Shakespeare play he might readily have echoed Wolsey's "Farewell, a long farewell to all my greatness" at this distressing point. There can perhaps be no real doubt that Carr's injudicious behaviour helped to contribute towards his own downfall – as Wolsey's did; it is nevertheless a pity that it should so have happened that the body-line controversy should have numbered him so decisively among its victims. It may well have been time that he went; but it was sad that he had to go like that.

This occurred in December 1934; in March 1935 the M.C.C. finally stabilised their attitude, incorporating into their Instructions to Umpires a set of rules that are still in force at the present time. Referring to the regrettable fact that the season of 1934 had shown evidence of cases where "direct attack" by the bowler on the batsman had occurred, and defining "direct attack" as "persistent and systematic bowling of fast short-pitched balls at the batsman standing clear of his wicket", the M.C.C., ruling that such bowling was unfair and that it should be eliminated from the game, instructed the umpire, on judging that such unfair bowling had taken place, to caution the offending bowler, inform his captain if the caution proved ineffective, and on repetition of the offence call "dead ball", conclude the over, order the bowler to be taken off and prohibit him from bowling again during the same innings. With the proclamation of these rules the M.C.C. virtually locked the door on the continuance and development of the tactics conceived by Jardine, although they never specifically condemned the system as adopted by him or his followers on the Australian tour or after.

There remained the necessary task of placating the Australians. The 1934 tour in England had done something towards this, and reconciliation, dare one suggest, had been something the easier since Australia had won the series and Bradman had (after a tentative start and a conspicuous failure against Verity on a wet wicket) re-settled into his reassuring gigantism; but the Notts match had not helped, and there were still international doubtings. It was therefore a very convenient moment for the already projected tour of New Zealand arranged for the winter of 1935-36 to be mounted in part as a placatory exercise, as it was designed to include not only a great number of fixtures in New Zealand that the 1932-33 tour could not possibly have found room for, but also, very valuably, a short run of six games in Australia itself, against the five States and an Australian XI. No Tests were played, and the touring party included an attractive collection of enterprising amateurs and good middle-of-the-road professionals, most of whom had attained or would attain Test standard in their own right but none of whom were in the very top rank of International performers. The captain of this companionable and resourceful party was Errol Holmes, who had succeeded Jardine as Surrey captain and who in temperament and outlook provided a most conspicuous contrast to his senior's dedicated austerities. A chivalrous romantic of optimistic temper, outgoing and engaging, he was primed before departure by the Secretary of the M.C.C. and told quite specifically that the venture was to be mainly a good-will tour and that the results were not to be considered as mattering very much. They were to do everything they could to avoid the "body-line" controversy while they were in Australia, and were to make active efforts to induce Australia to bury any hatchet still above ground by, so the recommendations ran, being cheerful and pleasant and playing the game in the proper spirit. Each member of the team – so the captain was told – had been selected not only for his cricketing abilities but also for his ambassadorial potentialities. And with this, and with the implied exhortation "Go in, but don't bother if you don't win", the skipper was benignly sent about his business, – and as far as the Australian portion of the tour was concerned, they didn't do so badly even over the results, as out of the six games there they won three, drew two and only lost one. The State elevens do not seem always to have fielded their strongest sides, but, at least, Bradman was among the few top-liners who turned out against them; and in the opinion of the captain, the team itself, and indeed of everybody else, the mission so far as it went was a complete and reassuring success.

The next winter, 1936-37, saw the resumption of the regular England-Australia series, the first visit of an English Test side to Australia since the great disturbance. With diplomatic effectiveness the captaincy was given to G.O. Allen, who had so positively dissociated himself from the offending strategies on the fatal tour, and it is clear that the mission enjoined upon him and his party was as much concerned with regaining mutual confidence as with regaining the Ashes. They succeeded without much trouble in regaining the first; but for all their varied talent they could not summon a sufficiently potent combination of concentration and good fortune to regain the second. In the context of the prolonged episode which has been the subject of this book, the mission may generally be felt to have had a happy enough conclusion. Neville Cardus, who accompanied the party, along with C. B. Fry for good articulate measure, has made it very clear that by this time the Australians were only too ready to make it up. They welcomed Allen's men with hospitable warmth, they cheered their successes to the echo and were even openly sympathetic with their failures. They readily received Voce as one of the party, no doubt enquiring solicitously after his shins; and Voce, less turbulent by now, having made a separate peace, and serene in the successful progress of his career, no doubt replied equally in kind. The Board of Control had apparently exercised themselves to control barracking, and the spectators, it seemed, made no difficulties about complying. "The games all passed off happily," says *Wisden*, "and there was a noticeable camaraderie between the two teams which enabled the matches to be played in the most sporting spirit imaginable." It appears that certain State bowlers indulged in a bit of bumping against the tourists, and that Allen conveyed to the proper quarters an intimation that if this went on in a Test match he might have to see what some of his bowlers (no doubt casting a quizzical eye in the direction of Voce and Farnes, and pensively limbering up himself while he was about it) could do in that line in return. If there were a hint, it was taken, and there were no further public signs of any private aggressions. "For this", said *Wisden*, "the whole cricket world must be grateful." Veils of discretion began quietly to be drawn by both parties to the rumpus; and life began to go on as nearly as possible as it had always done.

But Carr for one could not readily forget the crisis that had cut him off from his career in the game; and although his exit was a largely involuntary one and Jardine's ostensibly the result of a firm decision of his own there was not much to choose between their several fates as first-class cricketers. In effect their careers were ended, prematurely. It is true that Carr was forty and was perhaps past his best, but as cricketers' ages were then reckoned he had several years of useful play in him still. Jardine was younger, at the peak of experience and ability, thirty-four only; in pure cricketing capacity his loss was incalculable, both as captain and as player. In the confused atmosphere of those days their departure went undeservedly unheeded — unless it was, for recognisable if unhappy reasons, welcomed. These two gifted players, who had each given great pleasure of varying kinds in their characteristically individual fashions, disappeared with small thanks from the sight of a public that owed them more than they cared to remember.

But the man who was in a sense less responsible for the distress and the disasters than they were but was more intimately bound up with the catastrophe because he, under instruction, was the necessary agent of it all, how did he fare under these continuing pressures? Carr and Jardine departed; what about Larwood?

Frankly, Larwood was never the same again: the fact has

to be faced. After the end of the fateful tour the very great Larwood, one of the three or four greatest fast bowlers in the game's history, is lost forever, and is replaced for certain seasons by a simulacrum, a make-shift, a very good bowler indeed but not the same thing at all. For this the accident of the foot injury must bear most of the responsibility; the weakening the foot suffered on the iron-hard grounds made it permanently unfit to stand up to the remorseless hammering that a top-class fast bowler could not help giving it. Physical causes must therefore be assumed to be the chief reason for the decline of his powers; but I am certain that allied to this was a sense of grievance, a feeling of resentment that he had in a sense been let down by someone, that grew and grew, not always with easily recognisable causes but sufficiently potent to affect his concentration, his zest and even his physical fitness. Strains and *malaises* attacked him more often: by 1937 his appearances became less and less regular: in the following year he was relieved to drop out of first-class cricket. In a way it was the man who was less responsible than any for the crisis who suffered most from its ultimate solution. He had neither conceived nor directed its operation; he had merely obeyed orders, loyally and energetically. Carr and Jardine were victims, but in a sense this may be said to carry some recognisable justice with it; Larwood had more to lose than they had, his art and his livelihood, and he lost them both.

It converted him for some time into an unhappy man, it seems. When he left cricket, just before the war, he cut himself off from it, never went back, made himself a new career as a small-holder and chicken-farmer, brought up a lively family — then later became an almost anonymous shopkeeper in a back street of Nottingham, shunning publicity and his past. He gave up watching cricket: ("I was disillusioned" he said: I do not pretend to penetrate to his full reasons, and can only record that his distresses, whether they need have occurred or not, were clearly most genuinely felt.)

Happily there is a brighter end to the story, and it harbours ironies of its own — irony does occasionally, although it has not that general reputation, point an improvement rather than a deterioration. The irony resided in the eventual re-discovery of his peace of mind not in his home town but in Australia of all places; and it is very warming and reassuring to know that one of the prime agents to encourage and assist his emigration and to give him a heartening practical welcome when he had finally pulled up his family's roots and arrived there, was Jack Fingleton, who in the turbulent moments of the fateful tour had had as much to fear and avoid as any of his colleagues, and had reserved his complaints for the dignity of a reasoned printed survey. Against Larwood he had no ill-will at all, whatever he may have felt about others; and he was only the first — there were many others — of the Australians who helped to restore Larwood's self-confidence by giving him such a friendly reception when he arrived among them that bitterness and reserve were melted straight away — a parallel to a process which had begun in England some little time before when he had been made, in company with a number of other comparable retired professionals, an honorary member of the M.C.C.; and Jardine (who it must be insisted, never ceased in

his expressions of gratitude to Larwood) gave him a farewell
lunch along with a few old friends shortly before he left
England at which Larwood departed so far from his
self-induced recession that he gave himself the worst hang-
over that he had ever had in his life. And to set an agreeable
seal on his rehabilitation, he met Bradman again, first in
England in 1948 on the great man's last tour, and again in
Australia when he had finally settled there; and the meetings
substituted a salutary relaxation for the unhappy tensions
generated *for* the pair, rather than *by* the pair, on the tour of
long ago.

And, as a postscript to this lightening last act, it is
relieving to know that Jardine, some years before his too
early death in 1958, made a business visit to the continent
where his name had been so freely anathematized and was
delighted to find a wide welcome there too. It seems that
Australians may contract their passionate antipathies and
cherish them fiercely while the cause of them is still patently
alive, but that they do not see good reason to let them
outlive their day. The treatment in later years of both
Larwood and Jardine is among the more reassuring and
redemptive features of a tale that is not the happiest of its
kind.

*   *   *   *   *

Such then, the final state o' the story. So
Did the Star Wormwood in a blazing fall
Frighten awhile the waters and lie lost:
So did this old woe fade from memory,

Till after in the fulness of the days
I needs must find an ember yet unquenched
And breathing, blow the spark to flame .....

Fade from memory? Perhaps not: it has always been a
conspicuous event in cricket history; cricket historians and
commentators, followers of the game of all kinds ranging
from the fanatical to the casual — all refer to it freely and
off-handedly, it is an incident and a phrase and an idea that
they use like shorthand as historians in wider contexts
casually throw off such equivalents as the South Sea Bubble
or the Jameson Raid — events whose implications are
assumed, and perhaps not often examined or reconsidered.
Not that it was not talked about and written about, even to
excess at the time and after: prompting at times the very
reasonable question that has been put to me during the
compilation of this very book, "What's the point of
another?" The justification I put forward is that although it
has been described and criticised incidentally and at some
length, sometimes by people who were participants or
spectators and sometimes by people who were neither, no
attempt so far as I know has ever been made to treat it in
detail, objectively, in its historical context and in its context
of character and incident, and to look at it in, as far as this is
possible, detached and judicious perspective. The fact that it
occasioned what may have been disproportionate unpleasant-
ness, the fact that it did have the unfortunate result of
truncating and even closing the careers of at least three very
eminent cricketers — these might well prompt a more than
passing doubt as to whether a re-examination would do any

more than re-awaken old quarrels, recall some of the past
that is best forgotten. I am not convinced that this is
necessarily a conclusive reason for dismissing the episode
from our memories. I think it is a good and valuable exercise
to take as far as possible a studied and dispassionate view, to
restate the facts on which assumptions, which may be
mistaken ones, are commonly based. I have tried to set out
the story as fully and factually as possible, commenting here
and there when I have felt the need, trying not so much to
avoid taking sides as to take into account the natures and
temperaments of the individuals involved and considering
how they responded to the unusual stresses set up.

If I come to any conclusion of my own it is that the
tensions called out unusual character, courage and resource
which amounted to rather more than need·to have been
asked of players in a context of this kind. They gave rise, too,
to ugly and unpleasant emotional exacerbations which should
never have been risked. What seems to have happened is that
a highly intelligent and gifted man applied his intelligence
and his gifts to the devising of a plan by which the
fluctuations of certain international sporting rivalries could
be subjected to additional pressures within the bounds of the
existing laws of the game, and found himself able to use the
services of one of the most effectively aggressive cricketers in
the game's history in order to do it. As he saw it he broke no
rules: but there seems to have been in his temperament a
certain lack of sympathetic imagination, an inability, deliberate or otherwise, to identify with the other man's point of
view. An innate doggedness and determination, of the kind to
harden before opposition, allied itself to a naturally aloof and

autocratic temper to make him, once his mind was made up, inexorable in his purpose, whether that purpose was worth being inexorable about or not. It led him into disasters of which he could hardly have perceived the ultimate implications; it led him on to crassly stupid actions and decisions which it is quite possible a less gifted and purposeful man would never have dreamed of performing. "He broke no rules," said one of his team to me, "but he broke everything else." This, I think, was Jardine's failure, if you can call it failure; that he was so intent on his mission, which on paper he triumphantly achieved, that he forgot the human values involved. His ultimate salvation, if you can call it salvation, is that throughout it all, even when he did not have the full agreement and accord of his own team members, he kept – not his purpose, of course he would keep that – but he kept their loyalty; they continued, even Larwood continued, to honour him and admire him, even after he had unintentionally been responsible for wrecking their careers. He had, one is assured, a warmth and charm that in the long run survived the forbidding austerity. In the honest single-mindedness, I had almost said the fanatical single-mindedness, of his conduct of the task entrusted to him, he was short-sighted enough to convert the beautiful game, which he believed himself to be serving, into the temporary semblance of a war. It was perhaps a tragic necessity that he was ultimately one of those to suffer for this. But the game survived; and sufficient of Jardine's qualities are apparent in his actions and his performance to have made it possible that when he is remembered among cricketers, as he is whenever the history of what is great in the game is recalled, he is remembered with honour and admiration, and such errors of judgment of his as may for a time have flawed the enjoyment of it for players, spectators and all those who give it their lifelong love, are forgotten and perhaps forgiven. The scars of the body-line tour are surely healed by now; and it does no harm to remember again those on both sides whose courage, skill and resilience ensured that cricket would survive in a civilised form.

Australia Batting Averages in the Test Matches

	M	I	R	HS	NO	Average
D.G. Bradman	4	8	396	103*	1	56.57
S.J. McCabe	5	10	385	187*	1	42.77
L.S. Darling	2	4	148	85	0	37.00
W.M. Woodfull	5	10	305	73*	1	33.88
P.K. Lee	1	2	57	42	0	28.50
V.Y. Richardson	5	10	279	83	0	27.90
W.A. Oldfield	4	7	136	52	2	27.20
J.H. Fingleton	3	6	150	83	0	25.00
W.H. Ponsford	3	6	141	85	0	23.50
L.P. O'Brien	2	4	87	61	0	21.75
L.E. Nagel	1	2	21	21*	1	21.00
H.H. Alexander	1	2	17	17*	1	17.00
E.H. Bromley	1	2	33	26	0	16.50
A.F. Kippax	1	2	27	19	0	13.50
C.V. Grimmett	3	6	42	19	0	7.00
W.J. O'Reilly	5	10	61	19	0	6.10
T.W. Wall	4	8	42	20	1	6.00
H.S. Love	1	2	8	5	0	4.00
H. Ironmonger	4	8	13	8	3	2.60

* — not out.

THE AUSTRALIAN TOUR

M.C.C. Batting Averages in First Class Matches

	M	I	R	HS	NO	Average
H. Sutcliffe	13	19	1318	194	1	73.22
W.R. Hammond	12	18	948	203	1	55.76
Nawab of Pataudi	10	13	623	166	0	47.92
M. Leyland	13	21	880	152*	1	44.00
E. Paynter	11	16	538	102	3	41.38
M.W. Tate	5	8	157	94*	4	39.25
R.E.S. Wyatt	16	25	883	78	2	38.39
D.R. Jardine	13	19	628	108*	2	36.94
L.E.G. Ames	15	21	604	107	1	30.20
G.O. Allen	12	16	397	66	0	24.81
H. Larwood	10	13	258	98	2	23.45
H. Verity	13	17	300	54*	3	21.42
F.R. Brown	8	12	186	35	1	16.90
W. Voce	10	15	143	46	6	15.88
G. Duckworth	7	9	89	27*	3	14.83
W.E. Bowes	11	10	38	20	5	7.60
T.B. Mitchell	8	8	28	10	1	4.00

* — not out

M.C.C. Bowling Averages in First Class Matches

	I	O	M	R	W	Average
E. Paynter	3	32.2	7	71	5	14.20
H. Verity	25	325.2	119	698	44	15.86
H. Larwood	16	265.7	45	817	49	16.67
T.B. Mitchell	15	126.6	21	492	25	19.68
G.O. Allen	21	251.5	42	399	39	23.05
F.R. Brown	12	105.6	15	427	18	23.72
M.W. Tate	10	96.7	16	309	12	25.75
W. Voce	19	255.1	33	866	32	27.06
W.E. Bowes	18	209	22	838	30	27.93
W.R. Hammond	24	204	38	578	20	28.90

Australia Bowling Averages in the Test Matches

	I	O	M	R	W	Average
T.W. Wall	7	160.1	33	409	16	25.56
W.J. O'Reilly	9	383.4	144	724	27	26.81
H. Ironmonger	8	245.1	96	405	15	27.00
P.K. Lee	2	52.4	14	163	4	40.75
D.G. Bradman	3	12	1	44	1	44.00
L.E. Nagel	1	43.4	9	110	2	55.00
C.V. Grimmett	5	147	41	326	5	65.20
S.J. McCabe	8	92.5	17	215	3	71.66
H.H. Alexander	2	46	2	154	1	154.00
A.F. Kippax	1	2	1	3	0	–
L.S. Darling	3	11	5	14	0	–
E.H. Bromley	1	10	4	19	0	–

The averages relating to the New Zealand part of the tour are of less relevance and interest and I have not thought it appropriate to set them out here. Hammond had averages of 563 in the Tests and 310.50 for all matches; Sutcliffe had averages of 12.00 in the Tests and 9.00 overall. This is sufficient as a succinct comment on the value of the statistic in question.

England Batting Averages in the Tests against Australia

	M	I	R	HS	NO	Average
E. Paynter	3	5	184	83	2	61.33
W.R. Hammond	5	9	440	112	1	55.00
H. Sutcliffe	5	9	440	194	1	55.00
R.E.S. Wyatt	5	9	327	78	2	46.71
Nawab of Pataudi	2	3	122	102	0	40.66
M. Leyland	5	9	306	86	0	34.00
H. Verity	4	5	114	45	1	28.50
H. Larwood	5	7	145	98	1	24.16
G.O. Allen	5	7	163	48	0	23.28
D.R. Jardine	5	9	199	56	0	22.11
L.E.G. Ames	5	8	113	69	1	16.14
W. Voce	4	6	29	8	2	7.25

Also batted: W.E. Bowes 4* and 0*. T.B. Mitchell 0.

* — not out.

England Bowling Averages in the Tests against Australia

	I	O	M	R	W	Average
H. Larwood	10	220	42	644	33	19.51
T.B. Mitchell	2	21	5	60	3	20.00
H. Verity	8	135	54	271	11	24.63
W. Voce	8	133.3	23	407	15	27.13
G.O. Allen	10	170.6	29	593	21	28.23
W.R. Hammond	10	120.3	27	291	9	32.33
W.E. Bowes	2	23	2	70	1	70.00
R.E.S. Wyatt	1	2	0	12	0	—

BIBLIOGRAPHY

The documentation on this tour and its aftermath is pretty considerable; I do not pretend to have made use of it all. Appended is an alphabetically-ordered list of books that I have consulted, with apologies to any that I may have inadvertently omitted. Even so there are probably dozens more. Not all of these were specifically concerned with the tour itself, but there is matter in all of them that has some bearing on it.

H.S Altham and E.W. Swanton	*The History of Cricket*
Ralph Barker	*Ten Great Innings*
Ralph Barker and Irving Rosenwater	*England v. Australia*
Don Bradman	*Farewell to Cricket*
Neville Cardus	*Australian Summer*
A.W. Carr	*Cricket with The Lid Off*
J.H. Fingleton	*Cricket Crisis*
Walter Hammond	*Cricket My Destiny*
Jack Hobbs	*The Fight for the Ashes, 1932-3*
E.R.T. Holmes	*Flannelled Foolishness*
D.R. Jardine	*In Quest of the Ashes*
Alan Kippax and Eric Barbour	*Anti-Bodyline*
Harold Larwood	*Body-Line?*
Harold Larwood and Kevin Perkins	*The Larwood Story*
Arthur Mailey	*And Then Came Larwood*
Keith Miller and R.S. Whittington	*Bumper*
Eddie Paynter	*Cricket All the Way*
Ray Robinson	*Between Wickets*
E.W. Swanton	*Sort of a Cricket Person*
E.W. Swanton (ed.)	*The World of Cricket*
P.F. Warner	*Cricket Between Two Wars*
R.W.E. Wilmot	*Defending the Ashes, 1932-33*
R.E.S. Wyatt	*The Ins and Outs of Cricket*

and, of course,

Wisden's Cricketers' Almanack, principally for the years 1934, 1935 and 1936. *The Cricketer*, through 1932 and 1933.

INDEX